I0814502

To:

....

From:

....

Find Joy

A Woman's Devotional to Find True Joy in All Circumstances

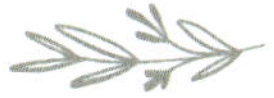

SHAUNTI FELDHAHN

Foreword by Alli Worthington

Christian Art
PUBLISHERS

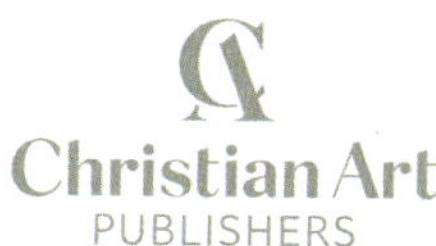

Visit Christian Art Gifts, Inc., at www.christianartgifts.com.

Find Joy: A Woman's Devotional to Find True Joy in All Circumstances

First edition 2024.

Written by Shaunti Feldhahn.

Designed by Christian Art Gifts, Inc.

ISBN 978-1-63952-765-6

Printed in China.

29 28 27 26 25 24
10 9 8 7 6 5 4 3 2 1

For Naomi, with love from the team.
We cannot wait for the day
when we see you again.

Foreword

God created us for joy. We have only to look at the beauty of the world around us to know that. Wildflowers in the spring, the sound of a baby's laugh, our toes in warm sand as the ocean laps the shore—these are but a few ways that I know God created us for joy.

As an author and speaker, I have the privilege of meeting and talking with so many women, and one of the most common threads among them all is the feeling that they are missing that daily sense of joy.

I certainly understand that feeling. I had a very long season where first my husband and then I suffered from a prolonged illness. There were very dark days when I wondered if I would ever feel joyful again. But deep in my soul there lived an understanding that God created me for joy in Him. Whether in plenty or want, in good times and in bad, in sickness and in health, throughout our lives, joy is available.

I discovered that searching for more joy means searching for more of God. I learned to see God move in my life. I discovered how to hear His voice in my prayers. And I fell deeply in love with all He had for me through His Word.

The more we see God move in our lives, the more we experience the Source of all joy, and the more we experience the fullness of His joy in full. And that changes us. We become grateful, forgiving, trusting, and confident in who He has created us to be.

Shaunti guides us on a beautiful devotional journey to discover the Source of all joy. In each devotional she challenges us, asking us to consider our thoughts in response to the things of this world and how

those things might be keeping us from the joy God has for us. She draws us to Scripture, showing us how God's Word is there to guide us back to Him.

This is a precious gift—a map of sorts—which will lead you day by day on your journey to Find Joy.

Alli Worthington
Author of *Standing Strong*, Podcaster, and Speaker

A Personal Note from Shaunti

"I bring you good news of great joy which will be for all the people; for today in the city of David there has been born for you a Savior, who is Christ the Lord."

— LUKE 2:10-11, NASB

Why is Christmas such a joyful season?

Despite the busyness and commercialism of Christmas, why do so many of us love that time of year? It isn't just the white lights that beautifully line the shopping avenues. Or the seasonal music dancing from the radio. Or the delightful chocolate-peppermint flavors of candy, creamer, and milkshakes that briefly appear in stores and restaurants, before vanishing for the rest of the year.

It is the presence of joy. Deep, expansive wonder. For a few precious weeks in December, real life holds its breath and a sense of heavenly glory invades the world.

We celebrate Jesus coming to Earth. We celebrate something that can never be taken away from those who follow Him: We are and will be living in the presence of our Savior forever!

Which begs the question, "Why is Christmas such a unique season?" Shouldn't our "real life" be lived in that sort of glorious joy? And yet it is so easy for our wonder, delight, and gladness to vanish as quickly as the chocolate-peppermint milkshakes. Especially in times of trial.

Good news of great joy for all people.

Yes, life can be very "real" at times. But so is the God who has invaded our world! In Him, we no longer have to struggle under the

weight of condemnation. We can be forgiven of the selfishness that infects every human heart. We can know that at the moment we step out of this world, we will be running into the loving arms of the One who created us, the One who came as a baby two thousand years ago—and of whom the angels shouted and sang. Their words have two meanings: that the news of His birth was joyous, and that He was born with the purpose of bringing us joy.

If our God wants us to live in that sort of delight, year-round, how can we do that? What would that look like?

It would mean we would have to really grasp His awe and majesty. It would mean noticing, remembering, and being grateful for all the wondrous things He does for us every day, rather than focusing on our very real challenges and worries. It would mean coming to hear Him, know Him, and trust Him even during insecurity, heartache, loneliness, or struggle. And it would mean letting that joy within us shine out for all to see, multiplying it even as we give it away.

All that and more is what we will be walking through in this devotional, as we practice the eight elements of finding joy that we can glean from both science and Scripture.

Sisters, no matter what time of year we are going on this journey, and no matter what is going on in our lives, let's ask God to guide our journey. Let's ask Him to permanently invade our hearts with Christmas wonder—and declare that we want to be both recipients and givers of His great joy.

— Shaunti Feldhahn

Elements of Finding Joy

- Live in Awe
- Practice Gratitude
- Forgive and Ask for Forgiveness
- Remember
- Trust with Confidence
- Hear His Voice
- Keep His Commands
- Reach Out

Day 1

Jesus replied, "I tell you, if these [people] keep silent, the stones will cry out [in praise]!"

— LUKE 19:40, AMP

The Mountains Are Shouting

A dark gray cloud hovered over our hearts and refused to budge. Two years after Jeff left his law firm to start a technology company, the market tanked. Just as we had our first child and I stopped working, Jeff had to stop taking a salary in an attempt to have enough to pay his people and save the company. Our finances were in crisis. For several months, we had to ask our church for help.

That summer, a friend offered his cabin in Colorado for some badly-needed "R&R." We flew out using frequent flyer miles and drove up into the mountains, talking through our swirling questions. How were we going to pay the bills? Should Jeff close the company, forfeit all the money we had invested, and start looking for a job? Should I put our toddler in daycare and get a full-time job? Things looked bleak.

In the background, on the radio, Andrew Peterson's song "Nothing to Say" began playing.

Just then, we came around a bend in the highway, and the most incredible, breathtaking vista of soaring mountain peaks rose up in front of us. At that moment, the music swelled and the chorus of the song rang out:

And the mountains sing Your glory hallelujah;
The canyons echo sweet amazing grace;
My spirit sails;
The mighty gales are bellowing your name;
And I've got nothing to say.[1]

We were struck silent. Miles upon miles of green and blue and purple, of snow-capped peaks reaching to the heavens. The grandeur of creation, shouting of a Creator. He created all of this—all of THIS!—with merely a word of His power.

Suddenly, we both had tears streaming down our cheeks. The same God who spoke this majesty into being loved us intimately; He had us and all our problems in His hands. Suddenly our problems looked so small compared to this demonstration of His power.

Friends, when troubles come, have you ever allowed yourself to be overwhelmed by the greatness of our God? We cannot feel despair and awe at the same time. That day in the mountains, our tears were not of sadness or even an overload of emotion. The emotion rising in us had a name: it was JOY. It was exulting, overwhelming awe at the majesty of our God. When we truly recognize the awesomeness of our God, we receive joy in return.

Reflect

Have you ever had an awareness of the overwhelming majesty and power of our God? If so, describe that moment. The next time you are overwhelmed with worries, how might calling that moment to mind allow you to trade worries for joy?

"A man can no more diminish God's glory by refusing to worship Him than a lunatic can put out the sun by scribbling 'darkness' on the walls of his cell."

— C. S. LEWIS —

Day 2

But whoever looks intently into the perfect law that gives freedom, and continues in it—not forgetting what they have heard, but doing it—they will be blessed in what they do.

— JAMES 1:25

Perfect Practice Makes Perfect

Growing up, I spent every spare minute in musical theatre: singing, dancing, acting; classes in voice, dance, drama. Practice, practice, practice. Whether theater or sports or math, "practice makes perfect," right?

Well . . . no. As legendary coach Vince Lombardi said, "Practice does not make perfect. Perfect practice makes perfect." Hard work itself doesn't bring the win, because you could be working hard at the wrong things. What brings success—in activities and in life—is working on and practicing the right things over and over and over. That goes for music, football, yoga, studying foreign languages, cooking . . . and living a life of joy instead of anxiety, discouragement, or stress.

Why? Studies show that doing something repeatedly forms neural pathways in the brain. The more we do it, the stronger and deeper those neural pathways become—it's like a new flow of water finding a path over the land, which then becomes a little rut, which eventually becomes a gully. Absent an interruption, that path becomes the default course.

Our thought patterns form pathways, too—both positive and

negative ones. We want to feel joy, peace, and delight, but we aren't always "practicing" the daily habits that lead to that.

That's why we identified the eight elements of finding joy for this whole devotional book, so we know what patterns to practice that will carve a path to where we want to be.

One of the crucial elements is gratitude. Not just the quick jolts as we throw up a "thank you, God!" because we finally found a parking spot (although that's a great start!) but the deep thankfulness that we are intimately loved and cared for by the Creator of the universe—the kind of gratitude that is unrelated to our circumstances, health, parking spots, or even whether we know where our next paycheck is coming from.

We also may need to take a hard look at whether we have dug an anti-joy "gully" in our mind and must create a better path. Here's the key question: what happens when we don't get our way or aren't in happy circumstances, and what are we practicing as a result? Is it gossiping and complaining to a friend or on social media? Is it exasperated eye-rolling or worried sighs? Negative chatter and a fretful heart are just us being really good at practicing the wrong thing.

When we purposely replace those reactions with a legitimate prayer of gratitude ("Thank You, God, even in this challenging situation. I know You're in the middle of it, and I know You will bring blessing through it"), we live in true joy.

Yes, sisters. Let's practice THAT.

Reflect

Stop and think about some things you're practicing (over and over and over again) that may not be the "perfect practice" God is calling you toward. Write down three areas where you want to start practicing differently. Say a prayer right now asking for God to open your eyes to how you can be truly grateful for these things.

"Habits will form whether you want them or not. Whatever you repeat, you reinforce."

— JAMES CLEAR —

Day 3

"[H]er many sins are forgiven, so she showed great love. But the person who is forgiven only a little will love only a little." Then Jesus said to her, "Your sins are forgiven."

— LUKE 7:47-48, NCV

She Who Has Been Forgiven Much, Loves Much

On February 3, 1998, I was watching TV, transfixed to hear the last words of Karla Faye Tucker, age thirty-nine. Her face filled with peace, she spoke to one particular family: "I would like to say to all of you . . . that I am so sorry. I hope God will give you peace with this. . . . I am going to be face-to-face with Jesus now. . . . I love all of you very much. I will see you all when you get there. I will wait for you."

Tucker was about to receive the death penalty for murdering a man and woman in their bedroom—with a pickaxe. Their family members, allowed to watch her sentence being carried out, showed the full gamut of emotion. Some were exhausted and relieved to be at the end of the journey. Others had tight jaws and bitter eyes. Who could blame them?

The crazy thing is how Tucker looked. For months, as the news had followed her journey, I was stunned by her open, joyful countenance.

Surrounded by barbed wire, she looked free. In prison, she had come to know Jesus as her Savior. She was overwhelmed with sorrow for how she had ruined so many lives. But then she heard the almost unbelievable truth: SHE WAS FORGIVEN!

Jesus had paid the eternal penalty for her sins. Yes, she would receive the civil penalty of death here. But she would receive life everlasting, saved from the darkness she knew she deserved. Facing that reality, how could she not be joyful? And how could she not pray for that same peace to come to those she had wronged, even in her last moments?

As the sentence was carried out and Tucker breathed her last, the news station showed pictures of Tucker from right after the crime, twelve years before. She looked like a different person; a woman whose face was hard, angry, hateful. The cameras turned to the family and friends waiting outside the prison, many of whose faces were hard. Angry. Then the news flashed an image of her peaceful, loving face as she waited to die.

The messages shouted from the screen. She who has been forgiven much, loves much. One who forgives, finds freedom. And when we find true forgiveness, we find joy.

Very few people are murderers, yet Jesus said even anger or cursing someone deserves eternal judgment (Matthew 5:21-22). How many of us have had bitter anger in our hearts? God says, truly, every one of us deserves death (Romans 3:10; 6:23). Once we grasp the depth of our sin and accept the immensity of God's love and forgiveness, it changes everything.

Reflect

Have you ever truly come to terms with the darkness in your heart and just what God has saved you from? It is so easy to think of ourselves as "good people" instead of realizing the incredible forgiveness we've been given. Jot down some of the little and big ways you try to get your own way, live your own life, and in the process, hurt others and hurt the heart of the Father. Then thank Him for His incredible forgiveness in Jesus.

And if you've never truly accepted His forgiveness and salvation, or if you're not sure if you have, see the prayer on page 246 at the end of this book.

"While others are
congratulating themselves,
I have to sit humbly
at the foot of the cross
and marvel that
I'm saved at all."

— CHARLES SPURGEON —

Day 4

And Joshua set up at Gilgal the twelve stones they had taken out of the Jordan. He said to the Israelites, "In the future when your descendants ask their parents, 'What do these stones mean?' tell them, 'Israel crossed the Jordan on dry ground.'"

— JOSHUA 4:20-22

Cross the Jordan and Remember

The moment finally came for the ancient Israelites to enter the Promised Land and experience the life they'd been longing for. But God's instructions sounded terrifying. God told the two or three million people—with all their animals and possessions—to follow the priests carrying the Ark of the Covenant and boldly cross the Jordan River.

Which was in flood stage. With no bridge.

It would be like every household in Cincinnati, Ohio, gathering all their things, stepping into a storm-churned Ohio river, and somehow crossing into Kentucky.

Can you imagine the people's skepticism and fear? Lord, I was already worried about how we would drive out the giants in the Promised Land. But how are we going to get everyone over there to begin with? This doesn't make sense!

We've all been there, haven't we? God has amazing things for us. Yet we're afraid to obey as we look across the churning water.

With the Israelites, the moment they stepped into the Jordan, the waters backed up. The entire nation crossed over on dry land.

Then God told them what to do next: take stones from the center of the river and pile them where everyone could see. Every time they looked at that cairn, they would remember this astounding thing God did. Which was essential, because crossing into the Promised Land wasn't the end of the story—it was the beginning. There would be years of efforts to fight the scary giants and follow God in the midst of a culture that mocked Him.

Sound familiar? But with each fight, each trial, the people of God could look at the pile of stones taken from the center of the river. Remembering what God did in the past would help them obey in the future. It would help them overcome fear and skepticism and replace it with a sense of expectancy.

Sisters, we may have no idea how God will accomplish something He's leading us to do. All we know is that He has something great on the other side. We need to believe God and not our fear, step into the water, and then watch what He does! Watch for each next step.

Then, remember. We need to memorialize His faithfulness!

It might be as simple as scrawling a few sentences in a journal. Or writing a few words on smooth rocks that we collect in a mason jar. The next time we are discouraged or unsure, we can go back to our journal. Or tip out and read those rocks. As we remember what God did the last time, we'll be far better equipped to trust and follow God the next time. It changes everything.

Reflect

When was the last time you reflected on God's faithfulness to you? What method will work for you to record what God has done? Right now, pray about it, commit to a method, and write that decision below. Watch your love for God grow as You remember what He's done.

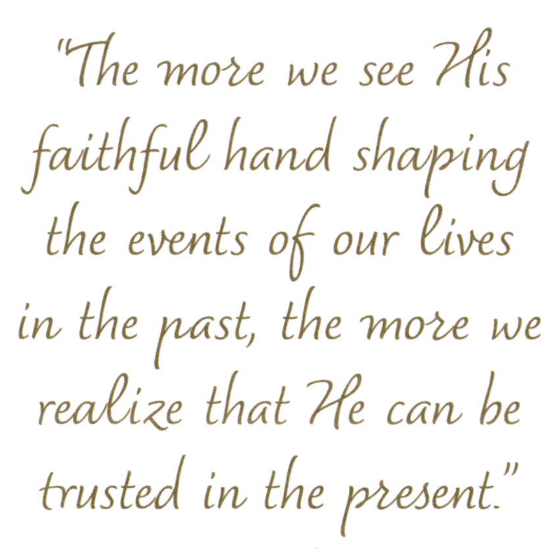

"The more we see His faithful hand shaping the events of our lives in the past, the more we realize that He can be trusted in the present."

— RANDY SMITH —

Day 5

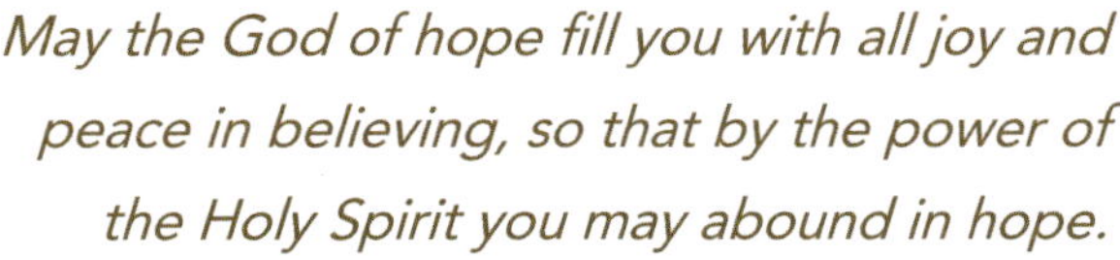

May the God of hope fill you with all joy and peace in believing, so that by the power of the Holy Spirit you may abound in hope.

— ROMANS 15:13, ESV

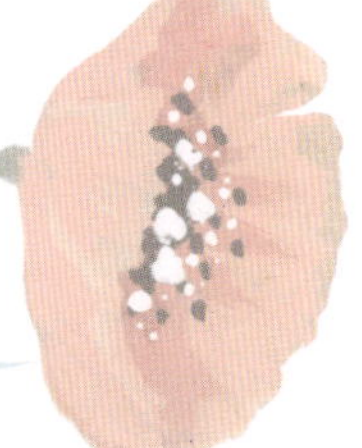

For Your Glory

Sabrina hadn't counted on infertility. But for more than two years, she found herself staring at empty windows on umpteen pregnancy tests, surges of panic and sadness swelling in her heart.

Before they got married, she and John had discussed how they would handle infertility if it happened; what fertility measures they would be comfortable with and their intention to adopt. It was all very theoretical. And now it was real, with medical tests showing no hope for change.

Sabrina was devastated. One Sunday at church, during a sermon series on prayer, the congregation was invited to post prayer requests on the wall with the promise that they would be prayed over. Eagerly, Sabrina posted her first prayer request and prayed with all her heart for God to open her womb and give them a baby. On week two of the sermon series, she and John simply wrote "Please give us a baby."

On week three, Sabrina knew she had to change her prayer. It was so hard. But she felt the shift in her spirit as she wrote these words:

If we're to never have a child because that will bring You the most glory, Lord, let it be. If it's going to take eight years, then let it be. If we're supposed to adopt, and that will bring You the most glory, let it be.

At that moment, for the first time in months, she began feeling joy. And it stayed. Her decision to relinquish her own desires and truly trust God with the bigger story of their lives—what would accomplish His purposes, not their own—gave her true, released joy in the journey.

Two weeks later, the senior pastor approached them. He had just learned that an unborn baby in the church would need to be adopted. They agreed to meet with the mother and the pastor for more information, and after they talked and prayed, they looked at each other and said, "We're doing this, aren't we?"

From that point on, they were able to go to the doctor's appointments and were in the delivery room to hold their baby girl as soon as she was born.

Sabrina and John later learned that their baby was conceived during that sermon series when they were pinning their prayers to the wall. It was when Sabrina finally prayed the prayer to trust God with confidence that the prayer was answered.

Sisters, this is a crucial element in finding joy in our journey. When we can pray the hard prayer and trust that the Lord is in control—with our families, our futures, and our hearts—the joy we receive is a gift that overcomes any struggle or heartache. It is born of hope. And that baby girl? They named her Joy.

Reflect

What aspects of your life do you find difficult to surrender to the Lord? (Hint: these can often manifest as worries.) Write them down. Then write a prayer affirming that you trust God is able to bring good through it and release those concerns to Him.

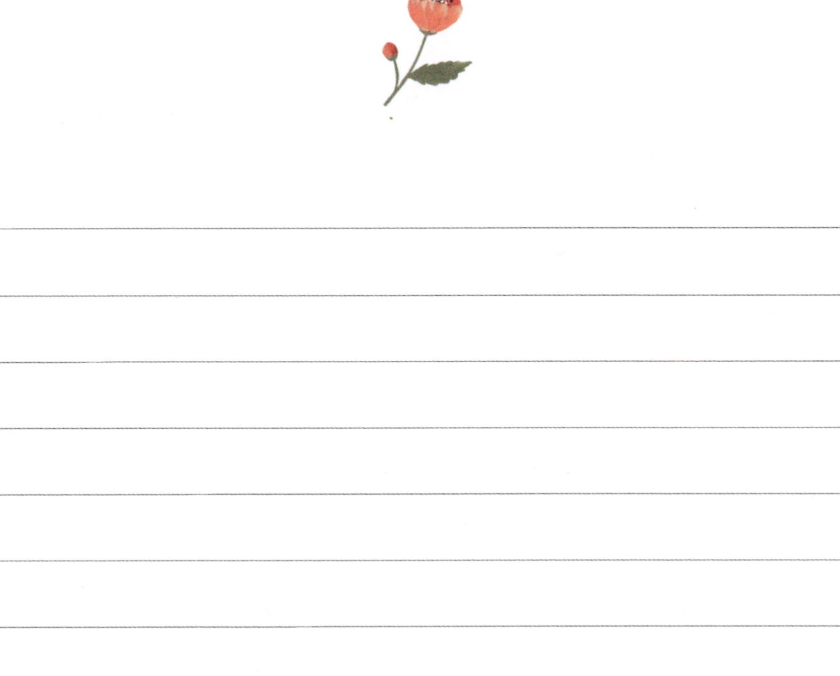

"There is only one way of victory over the bitterness and rage that comes naturally to us—to will what God wills brings peace."

— AMY CARMICHAEL —

Day 6

My sheep hear my voice, and I know them, and they follow me. I give them eternal life, and they will never perish, and no one will snatch them out of my hand.

— JOHN 10:27-28, ESV

Knowing the Father's Voice

I cannot watch the video without crying. Army Staff Sgt. Rob Cesternino had been deployed with the National Guard for nearly a year. His nine-year-old son Luca was at his routine Taekwondo class, sparring blindfolded with his instructor. What Luca didn't know was that his instructor had stepped aside, and his father had secretly taken his place.

As the boy continued sparring, practicing balance without sight, his father smiled, clearly proud of his boy. For a few more moments, he parried the jabs with a quiet encouraging word here or there. "Keep it going." Then:

"Come on," his dad finally said, grinning, "Is that all you got?"

Luca stood up straight, incredulous, staring hard at nothing. "DADDY?!" he cried.

Luca started tearing at the kerchief and blindfold around his eyes. He bent over, struggling, yanked them free, looked up with a gasp—and launched himself into his father's waiting arms.

As this boy dissolves into tears, so do we. We vicariously experience the indescribable sensation that erupts in the heart of this young one. This child was sparring in the dark and heard a voice that lifts his head. It makes no sense at all that his father could be standing there in front of him, but he knows his father's voice. And he leaps toward him.[2]

What is the sensation in this child's heart—and ours? Joy. Pure. Overwhelming. Joy.

Sisters, we may so often feel like we're blindly swinging in the dark. Another day, another routine. Another lesson. Okay, put on the blindfold and let's go.

And then. Do we hear our Father's voice? Some days it may be the merest of whispers. Keep it going. Some days it may be bold, calling us out, issuing a warning or correction. Other times, it may seem to make no sense, but we know He is calling us to have the courage to launch ourselves in a particular direction, and our hearts thunder in our chests as we scramble to listen and obey.

Sisters, in this life, learning the voice of God is a journey, not an event. And we will never hear Him perfectly. But we can listen. We can learn. We can watch for the quiet sense that I think I'm supposed to do THIS.

Then we can leap. It might seem so risky, but we can whisper, "Daddy?! Is that you?!" and then take whatever action we feel He is calling us to do. And as we watch what happens, so often we realize: Oh my! That really was God speaking to me! And as we do, not only will we be learning even more what His voice sounds like, but we will have the indescribable joy that comes from knowing we are hearing and following Him.

Reflect

Have you ever sensed God nudging you? Jot down what happened. If you can't remember ever hearing from God, don't be discouraged. You can hear His voice any time by reading the Bible—so do that for an extra few minutes now. Either way, write a prayer asking God to help you become more aware of His voice in your daily life.

"When our children were young, I'd sometimes speak in a whisper so they would inch closer to me. That's when I'd grab them and hug them. God plays the same trick on us. We want to hear what He has to say, but He wants us to know how much He loves us."

— MARK BATTERSON —

Day 7

As the Father has loved me, so have I loved you. Abide in my love. If you keep my commandments, you will abide in my love, just as I have kept my Father's commandments and abide in his love. These things I have spoken to you, that my joy may be in you, and that your joy may be full.

— JOHN 15:9-11, ESV

Obey vs. Keep

Have you ever stood over a crib and watched a newborn sleep? In the early years, I would often steal into the quiet, dark space of my kids' rooms. I held my breath as I checked theirs. It felt like sacred ground. And the joy and love I felt was too profound for expression, a deep well of thankfulness for the opportunity to watch over and protect these children with my life.

Jesus says there is a way to continue to live in that deep feeling of joy: Keep His commandments. He says that as we do so, we will abide in His love and our joy will be full.

It almost makes us ask: *Really*? Because we tend not to think of obedience as a path to sacred joy. To us, obedience may feel more . . . frustrating. Like staring at a cookie jar filled with freshly baked cookies and, by sheer will, keeping our hands out of it. Or maybe we see "keep my commands" as similar to an officer commanding a solider ("Sir, yes, Sir!").

It is stunning to realize that God's meaning is radically different. In this verse, "keep" is the Greek word *tereo*. It means to guard, watch over, preserve. *Watch over my commands, My child. Guard them as precious gifts in your life.*

Like a mother watching over her sleeping infant with a heart filled to overflowing.

We are called to keep and guard God's ways out of love in a world that cries out to us to compromise. We are called to know and hold fast to what He asks of us when our sinful, imperfect hearts are tempted to go our own way.

And what specifically does He ask of us? "My command is this: Love each other as I have loved you. Greater love has no one than this: to lay down one's life for one's friends. . . . I chose you and appointed you so that you might go and bear fruit" (John 15:12-13, 16).

It is usually pretty easy to love ourselves. To keep our own commands and our own counsel. Yet that way won't lead to joy. Jesus tells us what will: loving one another well in His name. Serving those we care about. Treasuring every opportunity to counter our natural tendencies toward stress, irritation, and impatience and instead live out peace, patience, and kindness in front of a watching world.

Sisters, let us steal into the quiet, dark, sacred spaces with a friend who is hurting, a spouse who is depressed, a child who needs our time when we seemingly have none to spare. Let us stand guard over our hearts to keep them pure. Let us see those times as moments to guard and treasure. And in so doing, Jesus promises our joy will be full.

Reflect

When have you found it hard to follow God's commands, especially the command to love? Write some examples below. By each one, write a line about what you might experience when you are obedient in these areas. Will that mean more joy or less? Ask God for His help to love His ways more than your own.

"[E]very clause of every commandment that ever proceeded from the mouth of God was divinely designed to bring those who would obey into the greatest imaginable happiness of heart. Don't swallow God's law like castor oil. For when you understand His intent, it will be like honey on your lips and sweetness to your soul."

— SAM STORMS —

Day 8

Let each of you look not only to his own interests, but also to the interests of others.

— PHILIPPIANS 2:4, ESV

Make a Difference to Others—It Will Make a Difference to You

An impossible mountain was looming that night, and it was all I could see. After two years of work, I had eight days to finish the most challenging research and book project I'd ever done. The deadline couldn't be extended again. I was exhausted and discouraged. How on *earth* was I going to get this done on time?

Then I got a tearful call from my college-freshman daughter, Morgen, who had just started final exams. She had three finals in the next two days . . . and was suddenly feeling sick and miserable, like a bad cold was starting. The drugstore was closed. What was she to do?

I prayed for her and suggested she ask if anyone in her dorm had one of those cold remedies that reduce the severity of a cold if you start it quickly. As we hung up, I tried not to let the worry about her overwhelm me. I had a major chapter to finish.

But something wouldn't let me start typing. Or, I should say, Someone. I started to feel this crazy sense that I should take a few

hours and drive to Morgen's dorm with some soup, ginger ale, and the medicine she needed.

I know it sounds horrible that I even wrestled with it, but I did. "But Lord," I said, "Surely one of her friends has a cold remedy!" "But Lord, if I take hours for this, how will I meet the deadline? Our finances for the next year depend on this book being published on time!"

As if God didn't know that already.

And I knew what God was saying. My little girl was feeling miserable. She needed the cold remedy quickly. But more importantly, she needed a hug from mom. So I waved farewell to my mountain, hopped in the car, and went to see my daughter.

When I got there, she broke into tears again and told me my visit made a huge difference. But I realized it was making a huge difference to *me* as well. My heart started to feel a sense of simple enjoyment of life that I hadn't felt in weeks. Funnily enough, it energized me so much that I was able to drive home and finalize that entire key chapter that night.

Sisters, we can stare at our looming mountain for so long that we take our eyes off of everything else. We lose the big picture. But serving someone else gets us out of ourselves. We are suddenly able to remember that we are the hands and feet of Jesus, serving at His pleasure and willing to be redirected to whichever mountain He chooses that day.

And when we do, stress is replaced by trust and an expectant eagerness to see how He will work. It brings delight. Allowing God to pull us away from our schedules and use us to serve others allows Him to minister to us, too.

Reflect

Have you ever pondered how interruptible Jesus was, often stopping to talk with a needy soul? Could it be that He was so submitted to God's rule over His time that it didn't seem like an interruption at all? Pray and ask God to help you surrender your time to Him in that way. Write the name of someone God might be calling you to serve, and how.

"Trusting God's plan is the only secret I know in the gentle art of not freaking out."

— LYSA TERKEURST —

Day 9

That is why, for Christ's sake, I delight in weaknesses, in insults, in hardships, in persecutions, in difficulties. For when I am weak, then I am strong.

— 2 CORINTHIANS 12:10

Delighting in Our Weakness

It was the moment I had been anticipating for years, and a catastrophe threatened to derail everything. But oddly, I was giddily excited.

Let me take you back. A few years ago, I was about to launch a new book on the Today Show. We'd had years of unsuccessful efforts to get on the show, and I was absolutely thrilled. I flew up to New York City the night before, fighting a bad cold but eager for the big day. I woke up the next morning with no voice. Full-blown laryngitis. I wasn't even hoarse; I literally couldn't talk.

Panic! I had had laryngitis before, and I knew my voice would come back in two days. But I was due at the studio in one hour. I asked my prayer team to bombard heaven.

Suddenly, I knew what Paul meant by delighting in his weakness and hardships. I could do literally nothing to get my voice back—it would have to be 100 percent God. My panic was replaced by giddy excitement as I realized I was going to see God at work!

Have you ever been in that situation? Where weaknesses, insults, hardships, persecutions, or difficulties make you sit up and look around in delight? No? Well, until that day, I hadn't either. Instead, we are so worried about our weaknesses, so focused on our difficulties, that we miss the eager anticipation God wants us to have.

But that day, I walked into the studio with an incredible sense of expectancy. I whispered a reassurance to the alarmed producers: "Don't worry, I'll be able to talk for the show."

"Um, okay . . ." They gave me the benefit of the doubt and returned to their tasks.

Still voiceless, I walked onto the set and met host Meredith Vieira and another guest. The producer counted down and the lights came up. And the moment I opened my mouth on live TV, my voice miraculously returned. Not even the remnant of a croak. (See it for yourself![3]) The segment over, I thanked everyone, left the studio, stepped outside onto the pavement . . . and couldn't say a word. Back to total laryngitis.

Friends, the only reason God's power and strength were so clearly obvious was that my weakness was also so clearly obvious. It was such an extreme situation that the only possible solution was God. But why on earth do we wait for the worst and most "hopeless" situations to notice God's strength at work? What joy we miss in the everyday difficulties!

Let's instead live with that astounding sense of anticipation, excitement, and delight that comes from expecting and thus looking for God to work in our hardships, every single day.

Reflect

Write below a weakness you have: a physical frailty, a character flaw, an anxious mindset. How might God use this weakness to show His power in your life—and what might you need to do in order to allow Him to do that? Ask God to show His strength through your weakness.

"There is nothing that moves a loving father's soul quite like his child's cry."

— JONI EARECKSON TADA —

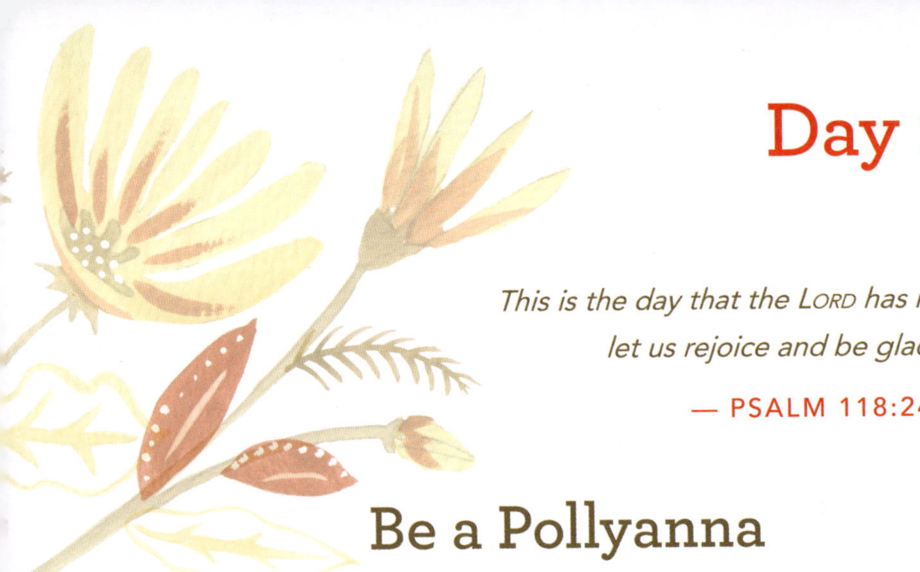

Day 10

This is the day that the Lord has made; let us rejoice and be glad in it.

— PSALM 118:24, ESV

Be a Pollyanna

One of my biggest pet peeves is when Christians say—as they are trying to avoid being seen as naively positive—"I am not being Pollyanna-ish" or "Let's not be Pollyanna-ish."

I always think to myself: *You must not have read the book. Christ-followers are supposed to be Pollyanna-ish!*

In the landmark novel *Pollyanna,* written by Eleanor H. Porter in 1913, the titular character was a young girl who was always glad, even in hardship, because the Bible tells us to be so. Her missionary father began teaching her to rejoice and be glad in all things one Christmas when the family received via steamer ship a barrel filled with random items a missionary family might need. Pollyanna wanted a doll so badly, but when the barrel was opened, there was no doll. Instead, there was a pair of crutches.

Pollyanna was so sad . . . but then her father challenged her to *be glad for the crutches.* Why? *Because we don't need them!* It changed her outlook completely, and she lived her life from then on, despite many serious challenges, with that attitude of abundant gladness. Which in turn completely transformed the people around her.

It's a beautiful story. And living in that "rejoice and be glad" attitude is what God directly asks of us, every day. Despite our very real challenges.

I watched this play out not long ago with a family who was walking a very, very hard road. Their son had a dangerous heart situation, with multiple surgeries, and doctors warned he might not survive. They knew they had a choice to make about how they were going to proceed. Walk in absolute fear (and the negativity that comes with it) or choose gladness and gratitude. Yes, things were very difficult, beyond what most families will ever endure. *But there were always going to be positive things they could thank God for as well.* They knew if they didn't proactively find them and express gratitude and thanksgiving on a daily basis, they could easily be swallowed up in the grief, fear, and pain they were experiencing. They coined the phrase, "Choose gratitude because it won't choose you."

Being "Pollyanna-ish" is not being unreasonably grateful, unreasonably glad, and unreasonably joyful. There's no such thing! It is the way God commands us to live. And in my research studies, I've seen the incredible importance of this mindset to living a life of joy. There is power in looking for the good things that God is doing, in looking for things that we can be thankful for—even when they're hard.

Reflect

Write down one or two things you have been fearful about or complained about recently. (Larger than expected electric bill? Extra work because a coworker called in sick? A demanding family member?) What can you "be glad" for about those same things? (You have a home that is comfortable despite the weather; your coworker did not share her virus; helping that family member allows you to show them love.) Commit to finding the good in the seemingly bad for one week and record what happens.

"When we bless God for mercies we prolong them, and when we bless Him for miseries we usually end them."

— CHARLES SPURGEON —

Day 11

I lift up my eyes to You, the One enthroned in heaven. As the eyes of servants look to the hand of their master, as the eyes of a maidservant look to the hand of her mistress, so our eyes are on the LORD our God until He shows us mercy.

— PSALM 123:1-2, BSB

Response Is a Choice

Emily's dreams had finally come true. She had married Nick, the handsome, charming guy from church. She had the house with a white picket fence and two adorable boys. Check the box on the American Dream, right? Wrong. Months after their second son was born, Nick abandoned the family.

Emily was shattered. And she stayed shattered for twenty years. Single parenthood and poverty were so hard. Although she knew in her head that God would provide and that He was in control, her heart had a harder time. Anger, bitterness, and fear swirled about the injustices and hardships she—and her boys—endured, through no fault of their own. It was especially hard because one of her sons was handling things reasonably well, but the other was self-destructing in drugs and despair.

She began overeating to soothe her emotions and was soon severely overweight. She developed fibromyalgia, then arthritis. She lost the ability to sleep without pills, then became addicted to prescription pain meds and lost her job.

Sisters, when we have legitimate grievances, it is so easy to rehearse them. And it is so hard to let them go. When the actions of others hurt us or those we love, the hardship is often all that we can see. We take our eyes off our Master and put them on the injustice. And perhaps without realizing it, we move from something unjustly happening *to* us, to actively giving the injustice the ability to *keep* harming us.

God calls us to a very different choice: to take our eyes off our very real trials and instead watch Him, on His throne, as closely as a servant girl would watch her master. Learning about Him, loving Him, and *expecting* Him to act in mercy will bring peace where there is bitterness and joy even in the midst of hardship.

One night, Emily felt God calling her to surrender, to lay down the anger she had carried for two decades, and choose a different life. In her mind's eye, she saw the two different responses of her sons. Both had been abandoned by Nick, but one had lived a life of anger, drugs, and rebellion while the other softened his heart, pressed in to God, and fought for an education. He was the only one of the three who had not let bitterness rule his life.

Her heart ached—oh, the wasted years!—but as she repented and turned to a new path, she found something very unexpected: the daily sense of joy and gladness she had been missing all those years. Every one of us can choose our responses to pain. Let us not give injustice any more of a hold, and instead glorify our King as we watch for mercy and fight for joy.

Reflect

All of us have experienced pain from the actions of others. Are you harboring anger or hurt toward one or more people? If so, choose today to write a prayer surrendering that anger and hurt to God and turning to a new path. Or if you have previously done that, thank God for the lessons you learned through the experience.

"Sadly, some folks want others to feel their pain, to hurt as much as they do-or more. My grandmother once told me to avoid colds and angry people whenever I could. It's sound advice."

— WALTER ANDERSON —

Day 12

[F]or it is God who works in you,
both to will and to work for his good pleasure.

— PHILIPPIANS 2:13, ESV

Don't Try to Figure Out Why

After a busy season of work, I was so excited for our family's visit with some friends who lived near the beach. Their neighborhood had its own adjacent private island and a ferry that would take us to the island each morning and back again each afternoon.

Our first morning, I was packing a bag for the family outing, when I suddenly had the oddest feeling: the thought that I should bring a tampon.

Wait, what? Immediately, my inner monologue fought back. *That doesn't make any sense. There's no way I'm close to getting my period.*

The feeling came back several times, and each time I talked myself out of it because it didn't make any sense.

In retrospect, although there's no way to know how the angelic realm really works, I picture a frustrated angel speaking in my ear multiple times, only to gesture, exasperated, at the King. "She's not listening to me!"

The reality is, I wasn't listening because I didn't understand *why* I would need a tampon. But the feeling was so persistent, at the last minute I threw in a feminine pad. I thought, *Well, I'm just going to be sunbathing on the sand, not swimming. If my period comes out of nowhere, a pad will hold me longer than a tampon would.*

We left the house and caught the ferry. Before long, I noticed a small group of college-age girls consoling a crying friend. I went over and asked if everything was okay. At first, they demurred, but I persisted.

Her friend gave in. "She's just started her period, and we don't have anything with us. We don't know what we're going to do. We might have to go back with the ferry."

My jaw dropped. Oh. The tampon. The tampon I was supposed to pack! I sheepishly explained, "I know this is going to sound funny, but I think God told me to bring a tampon, and I talked myself out of it. But I did bring this." I offered her the pad, and the girl's tears turned to joy. The thing that still makes me cry is what her friend said to her next: "See, Jeannie, I told you God takes care of you!" As you can imagine, the lesson that day wasn't just for Jeannie.

Sisters, one of the greatest ways to find a life of joy is to fully see how God is working through us. Which means we have to notice God's lessons and remember them.

Especially the lesson to take a certain action . . . even when we don't understand why.

Reflect

Have you ever felt the sense that you were supposed to do something that didn't make any sense? Did you do something about it, or did you talk yourself out of it? If you had the opportunity for a "do-over," what (if anything) would you do differently, and why? When faced with a similar situation in the future, how might thinking about your previous situation help you respond?

"Faith means obeying God, even when you don't understand."

— RICK WARREN —

Day 13

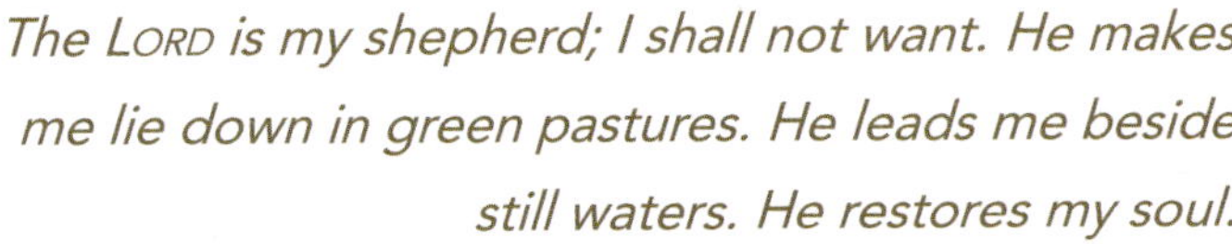

The Lord is my shepherd; I shall not want. He makes me lie down in green pastures. He leads me beside still waters. He restores my soul.

— PSALM 23:1-3, ESV

"Green Pastures" in the Next Step

Have you ever been stressed about finances? That's probably a silly question. How about wondering how on *earth* you were going to have enough time to get some crucial things done? Or whether you would be able to navigate a difficult conversation, day, or season?

All those worries are actually just one worry: *Will we have 'enough?'* And that question can easily strip away our joy.

Whenever we have a scarce resource—money, time, fortitude—we just wish God would give us a *lot* of it, all at once, so we don't have to worry. We long for what we see as the promise of Psalm 23, with the shepherd leading the sheep to an immense, soft green lawn. We picture ourselves lying down at our leisure, with everything we need for the foreseeable future. Overabundance. Easy mouthfuls of food everywhere.

By contrast, we see our own life of faith looking *nothing* like that. Instead: How are we going to pay the rent on Friday? How on earth will I be able to turn this work report in by my deadline? Will I be able to handle more months of painful therapy? We become

dissatisfied. Or anguished. Because we don't see obvious green fields of provision all around us.

But the readers of Psalm 23 would never have pictured that image. In a popular video, historian and scholar Ray Vander Laan stands on a rocky, dusty, seemingly barren hillside in Israel and explains that *this* is what the ancient Israelites called "green pastures"—even though there's no green in sight. But then he points out tiny tufts of plant life around the base of thousands of rocks, where small amounts of moisture condense.[4] A good shepherd will spot these "green pastures" and lead his flock along that hillside. The sheep will get a mouthful here, walk a few feet, get another mouthful, walk some more.

The sheep trust the shepherd, who always comes through. He leads them into enough provision for the day. Not for tomorrow, not for next week, but for the next step.

Friends, how do you feel about switching our view of the hillsides in front of us? Our "will we have enough?" questions can become an adventure—an opportunity to watch God come through. Our good shepherd doesn't mind bringing us to the edge of our fears because He is trying to teach us to not worry about tomorrow (Matthew 6:34). He doesn't seem to stress about delivering in the eleventh hour because He wants, above all, for us to trust Him. To believe that He has the joy of green pastures and still waters for us if we will only see them.

Reflect

How do you respond when you see a seeming "lack" in front of you? (Not enough time, money, emotional strength, wisdom, skill . . .) List a few recent occasions when you had those worries. What happened? How did God provide? Next, list one or two upcoming events that may trigger your worries. Write a statement to God, trusting that He will provide what you need this time, too.

"God has promised to supply our needs. What we don't have now we don't need now."

— ELISABETH ELLIOT —

Day 14

Teach me to do your will, for you are my God. May your gracious Spirit lead me forward on a firm footing.

— PSALM 143:10, NLT

The Encounter

"How am I supposed to know what God is saying?!", my daughter used to ask in frustration. In high school, Morgen was transitioning from the faith of a child who grew up in a churchgoing home and who went to Christian schools, to that of a young woman trying to figure out her own relationship with the Lord.

What did she believe? Was there really a God who cared so much He came and died for her? Or was He a more remote deity? Was He there at all?

Many of us recognize those questions. We go through doubt. Loneliness. Feeling alone spiritually, even when surrounded by people.

It is much harder to feel alone once we recognize the voice of Jesus.

At Morgen's senior-year "Encounter" retreat, the speaker taught on Moses, the burning bush, and recognizing what God asks of you. He said, "Ask God to show you if He has a burning bush for you—something He wants you to do." As Morgen prayed, she felt an overwhelming urge to call her cousin, who was two years older, a college student, and someone she adored but rarely connected with outside of family gatherings.

Morgen was nervous as she dialed. Was this really God directing her, or was it all in her head? Her cousin wasn't a regular churchgoer, and Morgen knew this call would sound strange. When her cousin didn't pick up, Morgen thought, *I did what I was supposed to do and (phew!) now I'm off the hook.*

The next day, the retreat message was on Peter stepping out of the boat and walking on water—once you know what God wants you to do, you need to take a step of faith and actually do it. She *wasn't* off the hook! She called her cousin again—and she picked up.

Morgen told her about the retreat, her prayer, and her sense that she really needed to call. Morgen asked, "Is there anything going on in your life right now?" Her cousin started crying. Her longtime boyfriend had just broken up with her. She was feeling stressed and alone. Morgen's call had come at just the right time.

As she hung up the phone, Morgen was filled by one thought: *SHE HAD HEARD GOD'S VOICE!* Taking the risky step to call had not only shown Morgen's cousin that God cared—it showed Morgen something that can never be taken away from her: God was there, speaking to her, and she was able to hear Him.

Jesus wants us to *know* Him, and that includes learning His voice. He says He speaks in many different ways—the Bible, godly friends, a beautiful sunset . . . and that still, small voice in our spirit. Once we learn His voice and follow it, we have the joy of knowing we are never alone.

Reflect

Have you learned how to hear from God in your life? Do you recognize His voice? Take time to be still before God and ask Him, "is there something you are calling me to do?" As things come to mind, write them down. Pray about them. Then, take a step of faith to do at least one. Note here what happens!

"Faith is taking the first step even when you don't see the whole staircase."

— MARTIN LUTHER KING, JR, AS QUOTED BY MARIAN WRIGHT EDELMAN —

Day 15

For all the promises of God find their Yes in him. That is why it is through him that we utter our Amen to God for his glory.

— 2 CORINTHIANS 1:20, ESV

Have You Given Him Your Yes?

On Father's Day weekend in 2015, Pastor David Hull was awakened by a loud knocking at his front door. Three somber-faced policemen told him that the Hull's beautiful twenty-six-year-old middle daughter, Jamilyn, had been killed in a car accident.

I was heartbroken when I heard this. I had recently spoken at David's church, and Jamilyn was our main contact. She was a vibrant young woman who served everyone and sparkled with the love of Jesus. I prayed for David, his wife, Jennifer, and their other two daughters, now shattered and coming to terms with missing a girl who would never marry, have children, or enjoy the memorable passages of life on Earth. The next hug they would give their bright, beloved one would be when they were reunited in heaven.

Yet they also began to see that God was using this time in a way they could never have imagined: to issue a challenge to His people. The challenge seemed to begin during Jamilyn's funeral service, which more than 2,500 attended and (due to her many missions trips) another 4,600 people watched online in sixteen countries. They shared what she had written after a trip to Israel:

> Gethsemane . . . it is the place where my Lord said "yes" . . . where He wrestled with His humanness but ultimately chose us. It's where He chose me.
>
> His "yes" on this Mount of Olives changed history. His "yes" made a way for me to be new. . . . His "yes" broke any bondage that would ever try to overtake me. His "yes" places me in the presence of a Prodigal Father. His "yes" forever changes my identity. His "yes" gave me life.
>
> His "yes" overwhelms me. It demands a response. I still wrestle with my humanness, but praise God that with His strength, I now have the freedom to say "yes" no matter what He asks.[5]

After the funeral, something extraordinary happened. Young people became gripped with the simple theology of saying "yes." to whatever God asks. Just *one* tattoo artist in town said he did over sixty "yes." tattoos in the months following the funeral. #WeSayYesPeriod began trending. And "yes." jewelry is seen around the country.

What about you? Is there a "yes, period" in your heart for God's presence and calling? Now is the time to respond to what God has asked of you. He wants you to live in the joy that comes from obedience, a joy that overcomes any circumstance of this broken world. As Jamilyn wrote, "My assignments in this life might change from season to season, but my calling will always be to say 'yes,' no matter what He asks."

Father, make us your faithful "Yes" women, walking in instant obedience to You.

Reflect

What would it mean for you to not only say "yes" to God in big life choices, but also in everyday things? (For example, laying down your pride, self-pity, or envy? Choosing to take certain thoughts captive? Being kind when provoked?) Write down below what you know God is asking you to say "yes." to. If you are willing, write a statement of commitment to Him.

"Joy has an origin and a Creator. The more I get to know that source of true joy, the richer life becomes."

— JAMILYN R. HULL —

Day 16

Anyone who does not love does not know God, because God is love.

— 1 JOHN 4:8, ESV

Every Life Has a Story

After a hectic workday, Andrea settled into her car and headed for home, where dinner prep, laundry, and family time were waiting. She negotiated the route like the seasoned commuter that she was, but vehicle after vehicle thwarted her progress. She rolled her eyes at the old sedan going ten miles below the speed limit and impatiently swerved around an overloaded truck. Suddenly traffic ground to a halt. Great. There was an accident up ahead. Dinner would be behind schedule, along with homework time and bedtimes.

Sigh.

Suddenly, Andrea felt compelled: *Look at the people in the cars around you.* Startled, she looked.

She saw the weary-looking businessman. The carpool of women talking animatedly. The elderly woman being driven by a younger man. I wonder where they're headed, she thought, and what's awaiting them? She was hit by the reality that the people "thwarting" her drive home weren't just obstacles in her schedule. They were *people,* with their own destinations and plans. People God knew

and cared for intimately. People she—and we—usually think of not at all.

Are we called to more than this?

A number of years ago I was speaking at an event in New York for Christian business leaders. One speaker, in charge of marketing for Chick-fil-A, showed us their new training video. So many businesses see customers with dollar signs over their heads, he said. So they created a video called "Every Life Has A Story."[6] It showed people walking into Chick-fil-A, and each one had words over their head stating what was going on in their life.

Over a young woman: "Immigrated to America when she was twelve. Recently received her citizenship." The man who walks in: "After years of fighting cancer, he is now cancer-free." The woman with two kids: "Single mom raising a family alone and trying to make ends meet." The idea was for Chick-fil-A workers to really *see* the people they're serving.

How often are we too distracted, too focused on our own agenda—our own *selves*—to really notice the people around us? Sisters, the next time we are impatient—in the doctor's office, waiting in line at the grocery store—let's make the effort to really *see* the people around us. Then ask: how would God have us treat those people?

Have patience. Be kind. Pray. Maybe even reach out and connect. In doing so, we will feel the joy of loving others the way God loves us.

Reflect

Do you find yourself rushing through your daily agenda without really noticing the people around you? Where and when can you make the effort to take a step back and really see the people God has brought into your day? Journal your thoughts and commit to being more intentional at noticing others.

"I tell you the truth, when you did it to one of the least of these my brothers and sisters, you were doing it to me!"

— JESUS, MATTHEW 25:40, NLT—

Day 17

Therefore you are no more a servant, but a son; and if a son, then an heir of God through Christ.

— GALATIANS 4:7, NKJV

Heirs and Children

One Christmas break, my daughter and I watched a cheesy-but-sweet romance movie about a prince and a commoner falling in love. I was unexpectedly struck by a plot twist when the handsome prince character discovers that he was adopted.

Upon the king's death, even though a grasping cousin was second in the line of succession, the handsome prince had first rights to the throne. But wait. Having been adopted, he wonders, did he *really*? Yes, of course he did! He was born a commoner but was loved the moment the queen and king saw him. Through legal adoption, he *became their son*. In the midst of chaos, he simply had to act like it and step into the inheritance that belonged to him.

The same is true of us; we are adopted daughters of the King of kings. God *adores* us! We just don't always realize it or act like it. So often, we act as if we are merely servants, doing what we can to curry favor with the Master.

Certainly, we must serve and obey Him—but from a position of knowing how treasured and beloved we are.

As I sat snuggled up with my precious daughter, I suddenly had a totally different perspective. How hurtful would it be if instead of assuming that I unconditionally loved her, she assumed I didn't? How hard it would be to see her feeling insecure, trying hard to make me love her instead of assuming that I already do!

Yet how often do I do that very thing with God?

We probably know in our minds that God loves us—so much that He died so we could be saved. But do we truly grasp, in the depths of our being, the unconditional vastness of God's love for us *as His children and heirs*? Do we live in the daily, consistent joy and awe of having been welcomed into the forever family of the King of kings? If we haven't, let us really meditate on what that means for us. *There should be no moment when that is not in the backs of our minds* and giving us a foundation for deep, eternal security and joy.

And if you realize: *I don't have that certainty because I have never really given my life over to the King of kings to begin with*, then start there! Talk to God as your heavenly Father. Tell Him you know you're imperfect and in need of His saving grace through Jesus. Accept what He has done for you, and give Him your life. (If you want an example of how you might pray, see page 246 near the end of this book.) Then start living in the precious realization that you are not a servant: You are a daughter.

Reflect

In Ephesians 1, God makes clear our identity as sons and daughters. Read through this chapter, and as you do, list below all the benefits it says you've received through your adoption as God's precious daughter. Pick a few of those items, and write what it means to you. For example, next to "chosen before the foundation of the world," you might write, "I feel so loved that God specifically wanted ME, even before I was born."

"Whenever you feel overwhelmed, remember whose daughter you are and straighten your crown."

— AUTHOR UNKNOWN —

Day 18

I pray that the eyes of your heart may be enlightened in order that you may know the hope to which he has called you, the riches of his glorious inheritance in his holy people.

— EPHESIANS 1:18

Point and Call

In James Clear's book *Atomic Habits*, he talks about the Japanese railway system and its extraordinary "Point-and-Call" system. To an outside observer, it seems odd to hear the train operators pointing at a light and saying, "the signal is red" or at the clock and saying, "the time is 9:27." But it has proven so effective that it has reduced errors by 85 percent.[7]

Because train operators are using their eyes, ears, mouth, and hands at the same time, they bring a heightened level of awareness to what could be a very monotonous and subconscious daily chore. By literally pointing and calling out what they see, they have prevented serious accidents in ways train operators have never been able to do before.

I love this idea for those of us seeking wonder instead of monotony and joy instead of stress. Seriously. We may not always do it out loud, but I can imagine us at work ("The printer is working today! Yay!") or at the grocery store ("I'm thankful for that coffee right there!"), mentally pointing at things that we often take for granted. Because if you think about it, those "taken for granted" things are actually great, great gifts in our lives.

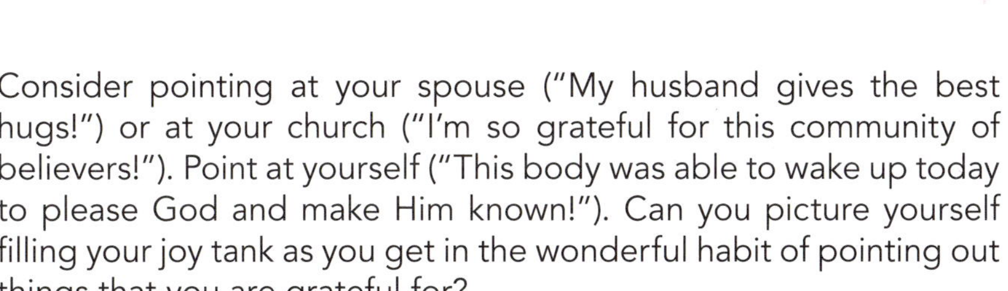

Consider pointing at your spouse ("My husband gives the best hugs!") or at your church ("I'm so grateful for this community of believers!"). Point at yourself ("This body was able to wake up today to please God and make Him known!"). Can you picture yourself filling your joy tank as you get in the wonderful habit of pointing out things that you are grateful for?

We so often slide into doing the exact opposite, don't we? It is so easy to subconsciously—or even verbally—point out things that are not life-giving. What do you think happens when we point and call out the disobedient child? And then ourselves for seemingly failing at this motherhood gig? Or the husband or friend who hurt your feelings with that insensitive comment? Or the fact that it's raining and you can't afford to fix the leaky roof?

Yes, in this life, there is trouble. But there are also gifts. If we don't try to counter our subconscious bent toward discontent, we are doing ourselves a huge disservice. God gives us good, good gifts, and it's up to us to see them. Let's be intentional about noticing the gifts God has put in our path.

Even in difficulty, daily joy is ours for the taking. All we have to do is point and call.

Reflect

What are you noticing today that is joy-giving? Point and call out five things right now that God has given you. Write them down. Then, as you go about your day, try to catch yourself when you are pointing out something that causes discontentment. When you do, stop and counter it by calling out something good instead.

"So much has been given to me;
I have no time to ponder over
that which has been denied."

— HELEN KELLER —

Day 19

The Lord GOD is my strength, and He has made my feet like hinds' feet, and makes me walk on my high places.

— HABAKKUK 3:19, NASB

Steady and Sure in Our High Places

A few years back, Jeff and I were driving to speak at a retreat center in the Rockies. We drove between towering cliffs into a secluded valley and gasped out loud. It felt like entering a paradise. A grassy plain spread in front of us, quartered by a burbling river and stream, surrounded by rocky walls.

As we drove around the perimeter, I gasped again, this time in alarm. At least fifty feet above us, on what looked like a sheer cliff, was a large goat. "Oh no—a goat is stuck!" Just as I began to wonder how to get a rescue operation underway, I saw another goat. And then another one. And another one.

Bemused, I thought, *How in the world did they get up there? How do they avoid falling off? And why are they up there anyway?*

I was quickly reminded of the verse in Habakkuk that says: "God is my strength, and He has made my feet like hinds' feet, and makes me walk on my high places." A *hind* is a mountain goat or deer: the verse was being illustrated right before our eyes. As I watched the

goats, I realized: they aren't afraid—they do this all the time! There were narrow paths along the cliff face, and this was where they were *supposed* to be. They constantly traveled up and down, back and forth, with total confidence.

To us, it seems scary. We imagine being filled with fear, balancing precariously on narrow ledges. But here's the thing: that cliff is not *our* high place. It's not what we're designed for. From the mountain goat's perspective, this is totally what they're designed for. Imagine the goat's freedom, the exhilaration of being exactly where it meant to be.

That can be us, sisters. Our high place is our own area of responsibility and purpose. It might look a bit scary to others (or even to us at first), but it is where God has called us to be and is what He's built us for. Whether it's a particular skill set, passion, job, ministry, role in life, or all of the above, our high place is something that someone else might find stressful, but which gives us life.

It also may be something we've avoided stepping into because we've talked ourselves out of it. Don't! Instead, ask God to show you if it is something He has built you for and called you to. If so, it might look scary at first, but your feet will be sure. You'll have the joy of walking in a way others may not be able to, and trusting Him every day—knowing He has equipped you for exactly this!

Reflect

What are you built for? What areas of life or ministry might make others exhausted or nervous, but really light you up and make you happy and excited? (Do you love speaking publicly? Homeschooling? Crunching numbers?) List those areas, thank God for them, and pray about whether God wants you to do more with those gifts and callings.

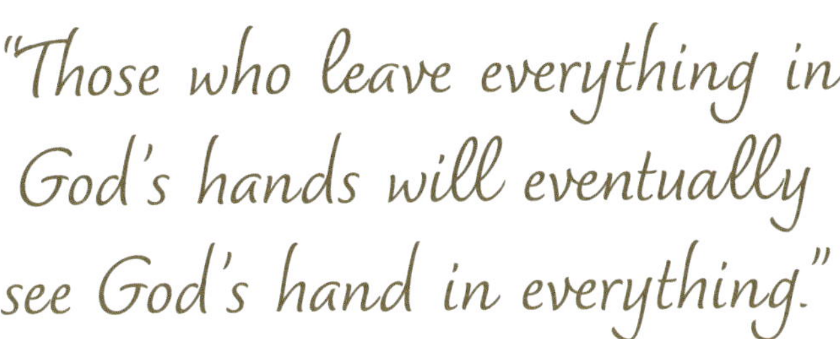

"Those who leave everything in God's hands will eventually see God's hand in everything."

— AUTHOR UNKNOWN —

Day 20

I saw the Lord, high and exalted, seated on a throne. . . . And [the Seraphim] were calling to one another: "Holy, holy, holy is the Lord Almighty; the whole earth is full of his glory." At the sound of their voices the doorposts and thresholds shook.

— ISAIAH 6:1,3-4

Holy, Holy, Holy

Have you ever woken up with a praise song on your lips or in your heart? Maybe it's stuck in your head from the radio or from church. Or maybe you've never woken up praising God, but would love to. A minister friend says that when we become believers, our spirit becomes alive. Our spirit is constantly in tune with God and constantly worshiping Him. What a beautiful image!

The bedrock of joy is coming to grips, in the deepest parts of our being, with God's goodness, majesty, power, and love.

Imagine for a minute the magnitude of worship in front of the throne of God, worship so overwhelmingly glorious that it shakes the throne room. I once stood in a stadium of 50,000 people all singing hymns together to God as the very walls echoed and shook with the sound. It was so powerful, I spent most of the time in tears of joy! And that is but a tiny, poor echo of what it must be

like when the angelic host sings "Holy, Holy, Holy" in the presence of our God.

The angels have a front-row seat to His holiness—and cannot help but worship. It is one thing to cry out about how mighty and strong and powerful a king is. It is quite another to *worship* Him. That means that this awe-inspiring God is not only mighty and glorious: He is GOOD. He is *worthy* of their worship—and ours.

It's easy to get sidetracked from worship. We get caught up in the chaos of life. Or we allow our moods to change based on how we feel at the moment. Or we get annoyed or sad when we don't get the attention or love of others.

But our eyes are meant to be constantly gazing upon the King. How often we forget that we were created to focus our attention on and worship our God. He deserves it, and we receive joy from giving it! If the first thing we think when we wake up in the morning is our to-do list, or if we even feel dread or apathy at the day ahead of us, maybe we need to get our spirit back in sync with our heavenly Father. Let's take a lesson from the angels and gratefully whisper (or sing or shout) our "Holy, Holy, Holy" to the Lord Almighty as soon as we open our eyes. By doing so, we can believe with our whole heart and spirit that the joy of the Lord will be ours. We get to worship a God who is worthy of nothing less than our total and utter awe.

Reflect

What is the first thing you do when you wake up? Check your phone? Pray? Sing? Grumble? Take a few minutes now to pause, close your eyes, and sing or hum whatever praise song or hymn comes to mind. How might doing that first thing when you wake up (even if it is in a whisper, so you don't wake others up!) help you connect more with God?

"Do not check in with the screaming demands of the world before you exchange whispers with God."

— LYSA TERKEURST —

Day 21

Create in me a clean heart, O God,
and renew a right spirit within me.

— PSALM 51:10, ESV

Turning the Tide

The popular rock-station DJ was stressed and agitated. On-air, he recounted that he was working a local music concert over the weekend, taking photographs of the band onstage, when a man started yelling and threatening him. Every horrible feeling this man had ever had toward a photographer seemed to be coming out. The anger was so palpable, the DJ was afraid for his safety.

Minutes later the DJ announced something shocking: the man from the concert had heard him and called in. Suddenly they were confronting one another, live, on-air . . . because the man was still incensed.

"I was there with my thirteen-year-old daughter! I spent a ton of money on these tickets, and you were dancing around, getting in our way, and blocking our view. It was ruining the experience for my daughter!"

"I wasn't dancing! I was in the designated press zone. And the stage was fifteen feet in the air—it was impossible to block your daughter's view." The DJ paused. "Why would you act like that?"

There was silence. The caller took a deep breath. And then . . . he apologized.

"I'm sorry. I just recently got a divorce, and my daughter is having a hard time. This concert was important to her. I'm sorry. It's just been so hard."

With that simple act of humility, suddenly, the tide completely turned. That pause, the deep breath, the humble apology for overreacting, changed everything.

The DJ immediately softened his tone. "I'm sorry. That's so hard. I didn't agree with your approach—I wish you would've just asked me to move. But I'm sorry. I'd like to offer you something. You can look at all the pictures I took at the concert, and find one you like—maybe frame it for your daughter? Would that be OK?"

The man could only whisper. "You'd do that for me? That was my daughter's favorite band. She would absolutely love that. You'd really do that for me?"

Friends, the act of asking for forgiveness in a heated moment takes courage, but it is game-changing. As is graciously accepting an apology. When we look beyond our own anger and pride, who's right and who's wrong, and humbly make a situation right, the tide *can* turn. A hardened heart can be softened. Relationships, mended. And anger turning to peace is a beautiful gift to everyone involved—even to those overhearing it on the radio while stuck on the freeway.

Reflect

Think of a recent time when someone was angry with you unnecessarily. Did you, in turn, become annoyed? Or were you able to find the humility needed to lay down your verbal weapons and respond in peace? Where you were angry and annoyed and needed to ask for forgiveness, did you? Ask God to help you respond to provocations with a humble heart.

"Venting is the world's foolish way, intensifying conflict. Restraint is the Lord's wise way, spreading shalom. And the Lord's way succeeds."

— RAY ORTLUND —

Day 22

And your ears shall hear a word behind you, saying, "This is the way, walk in it," when you turn to the right or when you turn to the left.

— ISAIAH 30:21, ESV

Be Willing to See the Steps

I sat on the couch for weeks, sunk in depression. All I could do was replay those horrible words from the Board of Directors: "We believe you are not the right fit for this organization."

Not the right fit? I had left Wall Street to run that particular ministry—and I thought it was going to be my career for the rest of my life.

With no idea what to do next, I dove into Henry Blackaby's *Experiencing God* Bible study, about hearing from God. One day, as I was driving and praying, I got the strangest feeling that the Lord was telling me I was supposed to write a book on a particular topic. I thought, *that couldn't have been from God.* I had never wanted to write a book. All I knew about writing was that it was impossible to get published.

Within an hour, I was reading Blackaby's point of the day: We so often limit God by not responding when He calls us to do something because we think we can't possibly accomplish it. Yet if God is calling us to do something we can't accomplish, then only He can do it—and He gets all the glory.[8]

I realized I needed to trust God to arrange what I could not, and in the meantime step out in faith. I would start writing, and watch to see if God opened up any next steps in front of me. Then I could take the next step that opened up . . . and the next.

Two days later, I "happened" to be introduced to somebody who found out I was working on this book. He said, "You're not going to believe this. Just last week, I was with a major Christian publisher, and they mentioned they really wanted to do a book on this exact topic. They said if I ran across anyone writing a book like that, to please let them know."

The book was quickly written, and it instantly became the number one bestseller in the Christian community. It not only steered important discussions and directions in the body of Christ during a key season, it also set the stage for my later books, *For Women Only and For Men Only*, which launched a ministry and research process God has used to impact countless marriages and families. If I hadn't been fired from that original job, it never would have happened.

Perhaps you, too, are reeling from a shocking setback or are confused about the next step in your relationship or career. Consider this: *Maybe God is using it so you can eventually accomplish something you could never have imagined.* If you sense God calling you to take a "next step," *take it*. Watch for the next step . . . and then the next. Pray and wait. No matter what ends up happening, what a privilege it is to watch His plan unfold!

Reflect

Do you feel God nudging you toward something too big for you to accomplish? Have you seen any next steps opening up? (Something like, "I feel like God is asking me to get into women's ministry . . . and recently women keep asking me for coffee to get life advice.") Write down today's date, then pray about what you feel you're supposed to do and what next step you see open before you that you're going to take. If you don't see any next step, write that, too, along with a pledge to watch for one—and then resolve to move once you do. Each time you take a new step, come back to this page, note the date, and write down what happens.

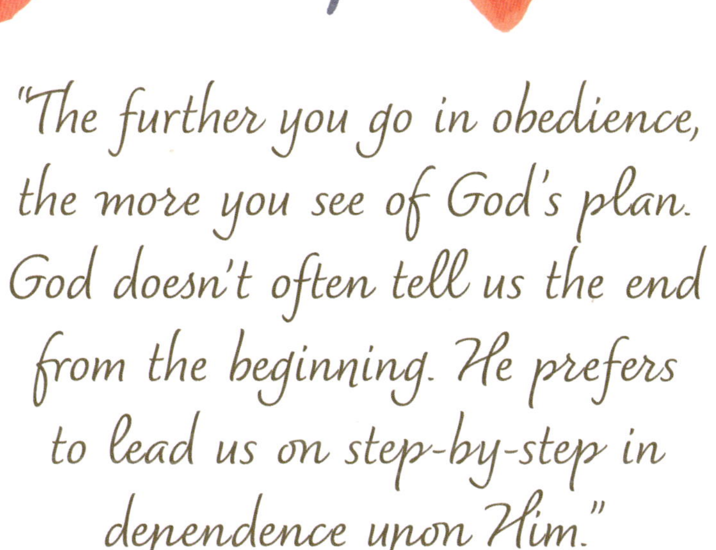

"The further you go in obedience, the more you see of God's plan. God doesn't often tell us the end from the beginning. He prefers to lead us on step-by-step in dependence upon Him."

— IAIN DUGUID —

Day 23

But then I recall all you have done, O LORD;
I remember your wonderful deeds of long ago.

— PSALM 77:11, NLT

Recalling the Lesson

Annie and her family had a hard time when her oldest child left for trade school. Annie, her husband, and their other children desperately missed Evan. They knew launching a child was God's plan, but they didn't know how to make it a time of rejoicing rather than pure sorrow. Annie got an idea: she began to casually pull out scrapbooks when the rest of the family was together so they could look through their memories. *Remember when Evan fell into the duck pond at the family reunion? Remember that Christmas dinner when the power went out and we ate cold sandwiches and played games by the fire?* They texted Evan their favorite pictures, and he chimed in.

It helped them remember: *Yes, things look different now, but our family is still a family!* It was such an important lesson. The good things of the past reassure us of the beauty in our future.

More important, holding on to memories of adventures, victories, precious moments, and milestones builds our faith. Look at David in the Bible; he often documented the goodness and help of his God.

When as a young shepherd boy, he strode out in righteous anger to meet the arrogant giant Goliath, he purposefully brought to mind how God had helped him in the past. He basically said, "God has helped me kill a dangerous lion and a bear, and He will help me do the same to this Philistine!" Another important lesson.

In the classic Christian allegory *Hinds' Feet on High Places* by Hannah Hurnard, the main character must follow the Good Shepherd on a sometimes-scary journey to growth and maturity. Several times the Shepherd leads her into situations that require great risk or sacrifice, and when she passes through them she prepares a little altar and keeps a stone to remember what she learned in each experience. At the end (spoiler alert!), she finds that the plain rocks in her pouch have transformed into brilliant gems.[9]

How do you document and remember the lessons you learned during difficult times? This isn't just a nice exercise—God says it is crucial for us.

Perhaps you make notes in the margin of your Bible or entries in a journal that you can look back on and remind yourself of how God brought you through a difficult time and what you realized about patience. Maybe you hang meaningful Scriptures that remind you of what you've learned about His goodness. Whatever your style, make altars of remembrance that capture what you've learned. These aren't just recordings of God's provision and protection: they become arrows in your quiver for the battles yet to come.

Our purposeful remembrances are how the challenges and beauties of life become priceless treasures that bring joy.

Reflect

Genesis 28 tells us of Jacob's commemorating with a stone pillar his vision of God and a ladder to heaven, saying, "Surely the LORD is in this place, and I did not know it" (Genesis 28:16, ESV). Since we could probably often say the same, let's look for God in the not-so-obvious. Think back over the last twenty-four hours. What gifts did God give you, and what lessons did you learn?

Remember

"[T]he secret to joy is to keep seeking God where we doubt He is."

— ANN VOSKAMP —

Day 24

So you received the message with joy from the Holy Spirit in spite of the severe suffering it brought you. In this way, you imitated both us and the Lord.

—1 THESSALONIANS 1:6, NLT

He Put You Here

Michaela worked in an inner-city high school, teaching biology to kids who didn't seem interested. The hours were long and the parents were uninvolved. Michaela found herself discontented, burning out, and on her knees, desperately begging God for a change. *Anywhere but here, Lord. Send me somewhere I can make a difference!*

Over and over again, she prayed for a job in one of the magnet schools nearby, where kids had hope for a future. She wanted to impact the lives of kids, and those kids *wanted* to be impacted. But the doors stayed firmly shut. She felt trapped in a job she disliked but couldn't seem to leave. Depression settled heavily on her heart. One day, as she began to pray, she felt a strong sense that the Lord wanted her to stop talking and listen. And what she felt she heard took her breath away.

Child, I HAVE sent you somewhere you can make a difference. I put you there for a reason. Stay where you are. And bring Me into your school.

Stunned, Michaela accepted the gentle (well, not-so-gentle) rebuke. She thought about how to "bring Me into your school" and decided to start a new routine. She arrived early at school the next day to walk the halls and touch lockers as she prayed for the students. Imagine her surprise when she found other faculty members doing the exact same thing! She had been so insulated, she hadn't known there was a community of believers within the faculty. Her heart swelled as she stepped into the life and support they offered.

She also decided to actively invest in the school outside just academics. She started staying after hours to attend her students' games to cheer them on. And theatre performances. And band concerts. Students started noticing that they were important to her, and it started making a difference in the classroom. Her heart swelled even more.

Suddenly, Michaela found herself *wanting* to take steps that had seemed burdensome before, like reaching out proactively to parents to say how much she enjoyed their children. Quite a few parents began communicating back and becoming involved in their kids' education. She realized that these families were not uninterested; they simply needed hope. They would invest themselves wherever hope was to be found—and they now clearly saw her extending that hope to their children.

It didn't take long for this previously low-energy, lackluster teaching job to start feeling positively life-giving to Michaela. The joy of the Lord swelled as she responded to God's call. And He says the same thing to each of us: *I put you there. Find the reason, and you will find joy where you are.*

Reflect

Whether you are a student, have a paying job, are looking for one, or focus on family and volunteering, how is your "work" part of God's plan? What are some ways that you can more clearly bring God into your daily work?

"Work becomes worship when you dedicate it to God and perform it with an awareness of his presence."

— RICK WARREN —

Day 25

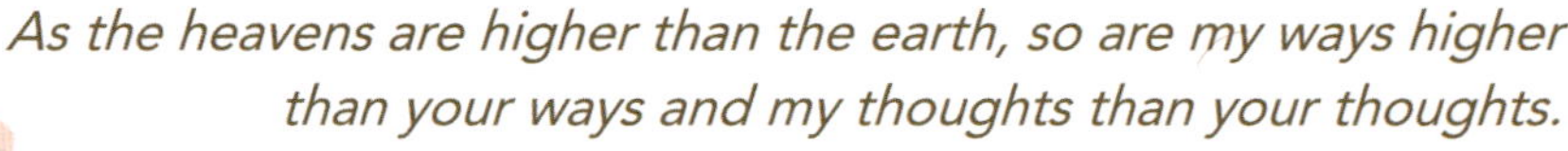

As the heavens are higher than the earth, so are my ways higher than your ways and my thoughts than your thoughts.

— ISAIAH 55:9

God Is Great and God Is Good

"God is great, God is good, let us thank Him for our food." It's a simple childhood prayer, but the first two phrases carry enough meaning for a lifetime's growth in faith. Because sometimes adult awareness of tragedy changes the clarity of childlike faith.

In 1996, when Jeff and I were newlyweds in New York, tragedy struck the city and the church. TWA Flight 800 crashed after takeoff from JFK Airport, killing all 230 people on board—some of whom were known to people in our church. It was devastating.

On Sunday our pastor, Tim Keller, addressed the question in every human heart during our darkest hours: How could a loving God let this happen? We are tempted to feel that the presence of tragedy (plane crash, divorce, illness, natural disaster, financial devastation) says God is absent.

Yet Tim shared a perspective that has forever changed how I see God's presence in tragedy. Do we believe God is big and powerful enough that He could have stopped the plane from crashing or prevented my loved one from getting cancer? Yes, of course—and that is why we are mad at Him, right? *You could have stopped this, and You didn't.*

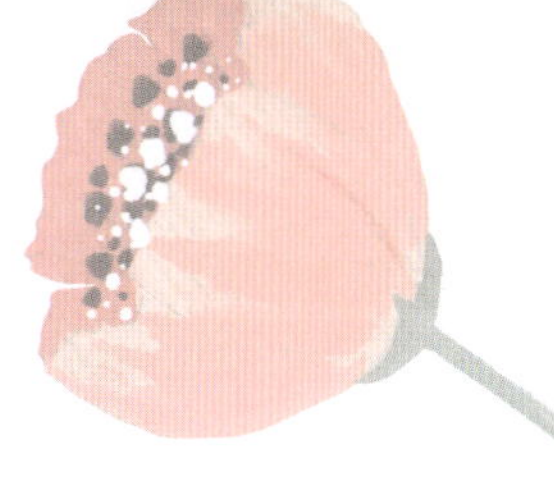

But if God is so big and powerful that He could have somehow stopped that tragedy, it would be supernatural in a way that our minds cannot understand. And if He is that incomprehensible, then *by definition we will not be able to understand why He allows certain things.* By contrast, if God is able to be understood, then He's surely not big and powerful enough to stop the plane from crashing—in which case, we can hardly get mad at Him.

His ways are far higher than we can understand. *God is great.*

Our greatest doubt, though, isn't really about God's greatness. It is about His goodness—about whether, when facing something we can't possibly comprehend, we *choose* to cling to a heavenly Father who loved us enough to send His Son to die for us.

The entire chapter of Isaiah 55, where God says His ways are higher, is about God's goodness and care for us. About the fact that this world is not all there is. About the fact that despite all the darkness of this world, there will come an everlasting day when:

"You will go out in joy
and be led forth in peace . . .
and all the trees of the field
will clap their hands."

— ISAIAH 55:12 —

A friend who daily faces a difficult life with grace told me she writes "God is great—God is *good*" at the bottom of every page of her journal. We need the reminder: God *cares.* We will not always know His ways, but we can know His character.

Reflect

During tragedy or hardship, have you ever wondered where God was? If He cared? When God's ways are incomprehensible, remind yourself of what you can know of His character. Read Isaiah 55: 1-3, 6-9, 12-13, and list every characteristic of God you see. For example, God is out-reaching, benevolent, a generous provider (verses 1-2). God surrounds the reality of the verse "my ways are higher than yours" with many reasons we can trust Him when our understanding fails us. How might reflecting on His character—the kind of God He is—help you walk through tragedy?

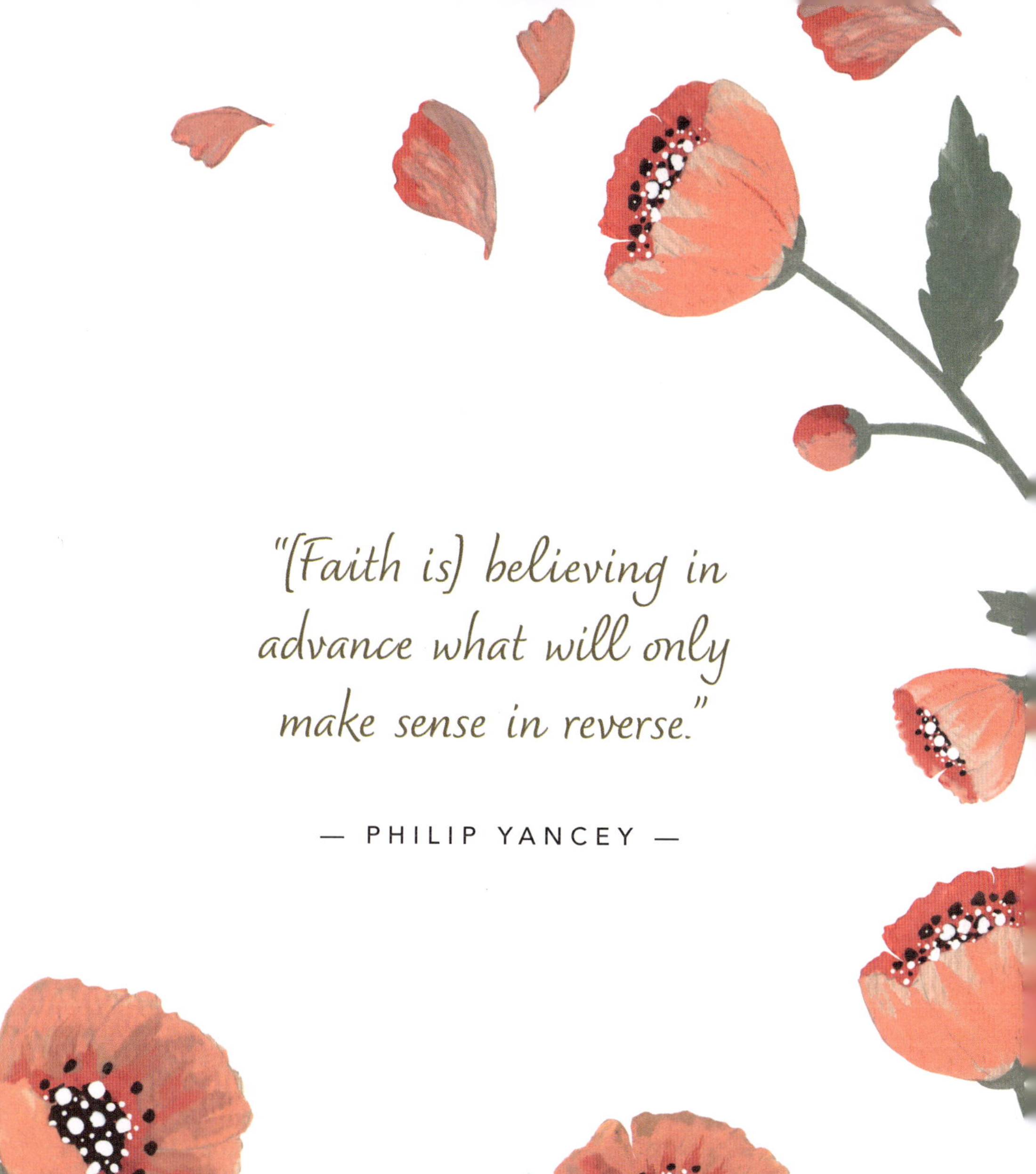

"[Faith is] believing in advance what will only make sense in reverse."

— PHILIP YANCEY —

Day 26

Let us not love in word or talk but in deed and in truth.

— I JOHN 3:18, ESV

Tune In

It was a really busy season. My kids were five and three years old, and I was finishing up the research for my next book. But I was also trying to shake off my former, Wall-Street workaholic ways. So I began working part-time so I could spend time with the kids after kindergarten and preschool. I knew that my "mommy time" would be interrupted by some cell phone calls and e-mails, but no biggie, right? I was quite proud that I was handling my multi-tasking with such finesse.

One afternoon I had just pulled out of the preschool parking lot when a phone call came in. I quickly popped on my Bluetooth headset. I was about to take the call when I heard the plaintive little voice of my three-year old son.

"Mommy, take your ears off."

"What?" Startled, I looked at him in the rearview mirror.

"Take your ears off." Luke mimed grabbing the earpiece and throwing it away.

At the time, Luke had an expressive speech delay, so he couldn't explain what he meant. But it didn't matter; I knew.

Day after day, he had seen my headset go on my ear when I picked them up. And day after day, in his little heart he knew Mommy's attention was not on him. And he needed my attention, not just my physical presence while I paid attention to someone on the other end of the phone line.

I knew God was presenting me with a profound choice: Who are you going to pay attention to? (And I sensed He was including Himself and His stated priorities in that question!)

Sisters, we've talked about how joy comes through serving others. And we know that if we've been given the gift of a family, we need to serve them most of all. But we may not realize just how much it means to simply give them our attention every day, in the day-to-day moments of life. That is our greatest service.

I knew what God was telling me to do. I pulled off the headset and said, "I'm so sorry, kids. I haven't thought about the fact that I wasn't really paying attention to you. Would you forgive me?"

After they both nodded, I said, "From now on, I will try to stay off my phone when I'm with you. And if I absolutely have to take or make a call, I will ask your permission first. Would that be okay?"

They both agreed—and not long ago, they told me how much it meant to them that I've stuck to that agreement for the last fourteen years.

But here's the joyful part: it has meant even more to me.

Your solution may be different than mine. But let's commit to taking off all distractions and tuning in to those who are the greatest gifts in our life.

Reflect

Who in your life loves you and really needs you—but doesn't get much of your attention because you are busy with other things and/or you find yourself taking them for granted? A child? Parent? Spouse? Friend? Write a few names here, then pray over the list. Pick one of them and start giving them more of your attention. If you think you need to do that with many of them, what changes can or should you make in your life to allow for that time?

"Life isn't a matter of milestones, but of moments."

— ROSE KENNEDY —

Day 27

Do all things without grumbling or disputing, that you may be blameless and innocent, children of God without blemish in the midst of a crooked and twisted generation, among whom you shine as lights in the world, holding fast to the word of life.

— PHILIPPIANS 2:14-16, ESV

Grumbling, Snakes, and a Greater Call

Have you ever dealt with a drawn-out, challenging situation that Just. Keeps. Going. On?

The Israelites' wilderness years were tough that way. Yes, God had delivered them from slavery in Egypt, but they were kept from the Promised Land. They probably felt like a bird in a mountain aviary made of glass: all that glory in sight, but out of reach. And one can get mighty tired of manna and water. Not to mention that for years their leaders were siblings who didn't always accept input from the Israelite community.

Input. That must have been what the Israelites thought they were giving, right? None of us see ourselves as complainers. In Numbers 21, the Israelites became "impatient." Come *on,* Moses, why do we have to go around the long way? And bread and water is prison-cafeteria food—which tastes terrible, by the way. So get with God on that, okay? Life back in Egypt was better than this.

Many of us see a little grumbling—against our conditions, against our leaders—as harmless. God appears to strongly disagree: "So the Lord sent poisonous snakes among the people [the Israelites], and many were bitten and died" (Numbers 21:6, NLT).

In the Bible, snakes often represent evil power or chaos. We would never want evil or chaos, but that is what "harmless" grumbling unleashes. It shows we have completely lost perspective about God's goodness. (We've been given supernatural food and drink! And miraculous rescue from slavery!)

Complaining also creates a vicious cycle by changing the makeup of the brain. Neuroscientists find that complaining releases the stress hormone cortisol, creating a "fight or flight" response. It also damages the hippocampus, a crucial component of decision-making. Specialist Dr. Travis Bradberry explains, "Repeated complaining rewires your brain to do more complaining."[10]

But guess what also rewires the brain? A thankful heart. Showing patience when all around us are impatient people. Speaking words of praise when others are grumbling.

Yes, our wilderness might still stretch before us. But imagine the difference if we lift our eyes to the free horizon each morning and say, "O God! Thank You that we are here instead of the many harder places we could be!" Each day, we can notice and marvel at the "manna" God provides for us.

Those long times in the desert when we don't see an end, when we are tempted to complain, are exactly when we need to be *most* attuned to thankfulness. Let's ask God to rewire our brains, shift our attitudes, and make us into grateful daughters who shine for Him—no matter how our journey unfolds.

Reflect

The Israelites' complaining showed a lack of faith in God's goodness and provision. What is the difference between a complaint and a prayer for help? Take a moment to think of one thing you're often tempted to complain about. Then list some ways you think God might want you to respond instead.

"Joy is wanting what you've been given."

— JOHN H. PUTNAM —

You, Lord, are forgiving and good,
abounding in love to all who call to you.

— PSALM 86:5

To Err Is Human, to Ask for Forgiveness Is Divine

We've all been hurt by a zinger from someone. The sarcastic one-liner you pretend to laugh at that humiliates you in front of your colleagues. Your sister's angry response to your concern about her health that ends with, "Well, at least *I* lost the baby weight!" The friend's "joke" that hits a little too close to home.

We've all been on the receiving end. But what do we do when *we* are the culprits, when we've been the one to hurl insensitive words in anger? Or when our mouths have jumped ahead of our brain, with hurtful results?

There's a clear answer . . . and yet we often do everything we can to avoid it. It can be awkward and painful to humble ourselves and ask for forgiveness. But if we don't, the other person being hurt is ourselves.

One of my closest college friends, whom I'll call Allie, dreamt of being a mom. But at the age of twenty-two, she went in for

routine surgery to remove a uterine cyst and woke up having had a hysterectomy. Our group of friends was devastated for her, but she recovered.

Two years later we were all together again for a wedding, joking with the bride, who had always said that when she was delivering a baby, she would tell her husband, "It's all your fault!" as she writhed in pain. Laughing along with everybody else, I joked that *all* the women in the group would be blaming their husbands at that point.

Allie looked at me and said, "Well, I won't have to worry about that, will I?"

I was flooded with shock, shame, and guilt. I sure hadn't been thinking about her situation when I made that joke.

It might sound odd, but I felt so terrible about how badly I must have hurt Allie that I began to pull away. I knew I should talk to her about what happened, but I was too embarrassed. We still saw each other, but I was putting distance between us. Several years later, together for another wedding, I finally found the courage to apologize. I told her it had been eating me up for three years.

She said, "Oh my goodness, you need to be released from that!" I started bawling, and the burden of guilt was lifted.

It's *so* easy to carelessly say or do something that wounds a loved one. We may think avoiding addressing it will make us feel better, because we don't like conflict or because we think dredging it up will make things worse. But waiting does the opposite. It saps the joy from our relationship. Instead, the healing balm of forgiveness can be ours—if we simply ask.

Reflect

Is there someone you need to ask for forgiveness? Write down that name, what it is you need forgiveness for, and when you feel you should ask for it. Perhaps even write a note to them—either to share directly or to guide your conversation when you feel it is time. If you are fearful, ask for help from the true source of all forgiveness.

"It's not how we make mistakes, but how we correct them that defines us."

— RACHEL WOLCHIN —

Day 29

The steadfast love of the Lord never ceases; his mercies never come to an end; they are new every morning; great is your faithfulness.

— LAMENTATIONS 3:22-23, ESV

The Antidote for Discouragement

As you now know, Jeff and I have experienced ups and downs financially. We've had seasons of significant financial challenges and seasons of great abundance.

I like the abundance better.

In the lean seasons, it is so easy to become anxious and fearful, isn't it? Are we going to make it? *How* are we going to make it? The mortgage or rent or gas bill is due on Friday, and we are already overdue on the phone service. Our minds can spin fearful scenarios.

But if we look for it, those times are also when God provides something far more important than just money. He provides the antidote for financial discouragement: the memory of a time when He miraculously gave us what we need.

When we really think about it, each of us probably have dozens—*hundreds!*—of such stories. And each is given not just for that moment, but to call to mind down the road.

For me, I especially think about the "$3,200 story." After Jeff had to shut his first company down, we had a toddler, a mortgage, and little income. Jeff was scrambling for legal work, and I was scrambling for freelance consulting work. We cut our expenses drastically and used up our emergency savings, but it wasn't enough.

So you can imagine our horror when we received a notice that due to an old tax error, we suddenly owed $3,200. It may as well have been $1 million! It was devastating.

A few days later, depressed and anxious, I opened the mail to find a $3,200 check from an old friend. The donor had no way of knowing the amount we needed, but said he felt like God was asking him to send it. Jeff and I broke down in tears . . . and have remembered it ever since.

So a few years ago, when we realized that our son's necessary epilepsy medicine was going to be an impossible $1,000 a month, we didn't panic—*we remembered.* We reminded ourselves that God has provided before. We can trust Him now. Great is His faithfulness! Shortly thereafter God provided: not with $12,000 a year, but by miraculously arranging for us to be part of the pharmaceutical company's support system and get the medicine for free.

A few years later, as I write this, it is likely that support system is going away, and yet I'm not freaking out. Because I *remember.*

How about you? What is your need today? Remind yourself of His faithfulness in the past: it is the best antidote for anxiety about the future.

Reflect

Whether you are in a season of abundance or need, make a list of a few ways that God has provided for you in this time and then thank Him for it. When you experience moments of want or doubt, look back at this list and remember how God has provided for you and know confidently that He will again.

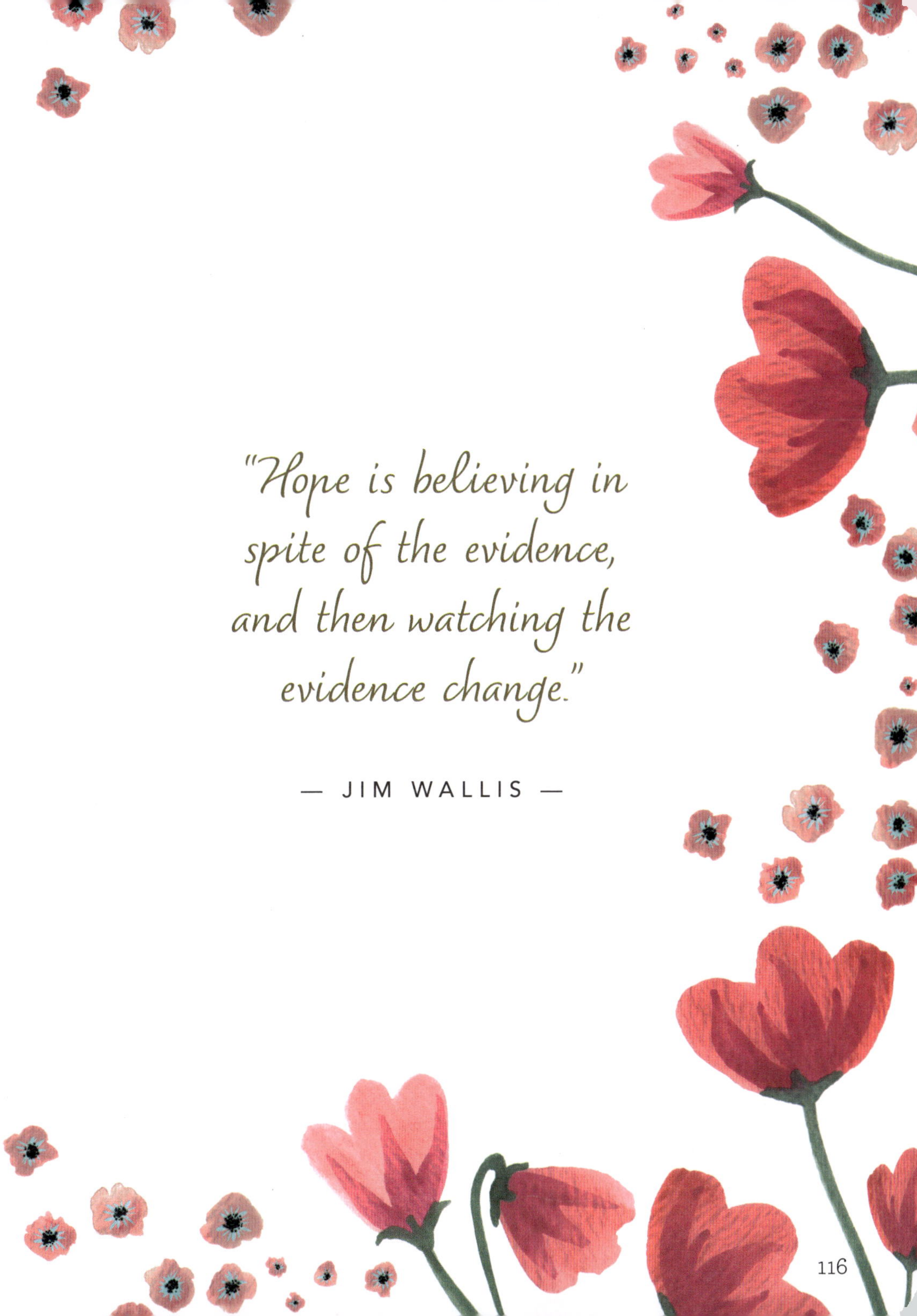

"Hope is believing in spite of the evidence, and then watching the evidence change."

— JIM WALLIS —

Day 30

For to me, to live is Christ and to die is gain.

— PHILIPPIANS 1:21

The Power of Fearlessness

Years ago, our beloved pastor and his wife and kids moved away to plant churches in the Middle East. Because of the leadership gifts God gave them, and His anointing over their life and work, their ministry very quickly bore great fruit. There were hundreds—thousands—coming to know the Lord in a very closed area.

Then came the night that the pastor and his wife woke up to see their bed surrounded by men wearing hoods and carrying hatchets. Their children were able to escape, but our friends were violently beaten. The wife had to be Life-Flighted to another country, and then back to the US, where she spent one year learning to walk and talk again.

At this point, one would think that this would be the end of their outreach in the area. But I can still remember tears rushing to my eyes when I read the wife's prayer updates. She was deeply anxious to get better . . . so they could go back! Her joy and hope in Jesus spilled off the page.

It is easy to wonder: *HOW?* How, in such deep trials, could they have joy? How could they *want* to go back?

The family did return, God continued to bless their efforts, and years later they ended up becoming the leaders of one of the most impactful evangelism ministries in the world.

Not long ago, when we were traveling near their US headquarters, we got together for dinner. We wanted our children to hear the miraculous stories of how they watched God work, time after time. We asked the couple, "You've seen God accomplish the most amazing things. What's the most important factor in why you've seen His hand move in these ways?"

The husband shrugged and said, "Well, it's amazing what you can do if you're not afraid to die."

We were silenced.

That really is it, isn't it? If we are not afraid, God can use us to do *anything.* Yet how many of us can say we're not afraid to make someone angry or to have a difficult confrontation with a friend—much less afraid to die?! A lot of the time, I'm afraid enough of someone's mere *displeasure* that it makes me want to placate, avoid things, and keep the status quo! And yet, that path will never lead to true joy.

God has a higher calling for the citizens of heaven. If we long for the joy that comes from God using us in mighty ways, let us be willing to act *like* citizens of heaven. It is amazing what God can do if we are not afraid.

Reflect

Proverbs 29:25 tells us, "Fear of man will prove to be a snare, but whoever trusts in the Lord is kept safe." What fears might be a "snare" for you—something tripping you up and keeping you from being fully used by God in the lives of others? List those below. Pray about and write down how you might address one of those this week.

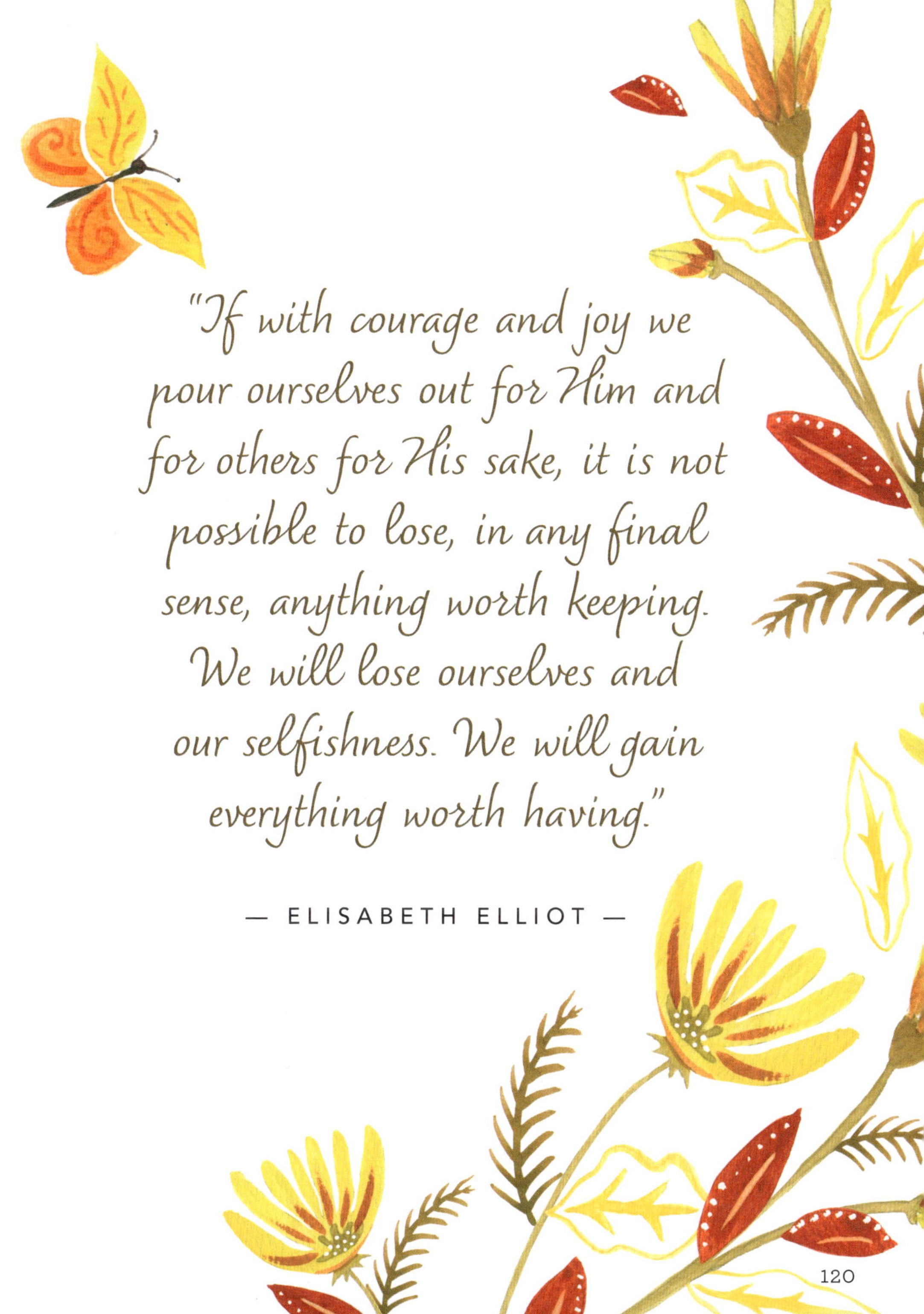

"If with courage and joy we pour ourselves out for Him and for others for His sake, it is not possible to lose, in any final sense, anything worth keeping. We will lose ourselves and our selfishness. We will gain everything worth having."

— ELISABETH ELLIOT —

Day 31

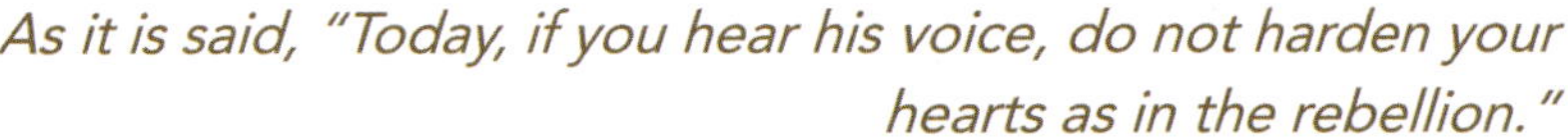

As it is said, "Today, if you hear his voice, do not harden your hearts as in the rebellion."

— HEBREWS 3:15, ESV

Give Them Your Boots

Kate was shopping at a local Goodwill store when she found herself distracted by two women trying on shoes—which was strange, because she had no reason to watch them. It was almost like God was bringing them to her attention.

She couldn't really hear them talking, but it seemed that one of the women urgently needed a pair of boots to fit. And suddenly, Kate felt a soft buzzing in her chest.

Give them your boots, she sensed.

What in the world? Why would God ask her to give a total stranger her boots? Especially since she hadn't even interacted with them. And on this rainy day, she was wearing her beloved brown-and-pink polka-dotted rain boots—the ones she always received compliments on.

But her chest continued to buzz, and she couldn't stop watching these women. She didn't know their story, but there was an undeniable need as the women frantically tried to come up with a solution. And she kept hearing that still, small voice:

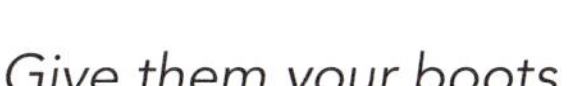

Give them your boots.

But that's so weird, God, she argued. *What would they say if I just walked up to them and offered them my boots? What if they don't even need them?* She imagined herself walking up to total strangers and saying, "Hey, ladies! God told me to give you my boots. I don't normally take off articles of clothing and hand them out in public, but I really sensed I should give these to you."

Kate tried to ignore it. She *knew* what God was asking her to do but stalled and rationalized as the women went up to the register.

As soon as the women walked out of the store, Kate didn't feel the relief she was expecting. She felt despair. She almost started crying right there in the middle of the store.

Even though it didn't make any sense, she knew God had been speaking to *her.* And now all she felt was an emptiness where there could've been joy—real, authentic joy that comes from the awesome privilege of hearing from and obeying the King of kings.

Unfortunately, as imperfect people, we may learn to hear God's voice only *after* we know we have messed up. We may learn to obey only *after* we feel the natural consequences of shutting our ears to His call. Which means that we need to be watching for second chances from our merciful Father.

A few weeks later, Kate felt God whisper in her ear about offering help to a family at their preschool. You'd better believe she jumped at the opportunity. Sisters, let's not miss out on the joy of responding to God's commands!

Reflect

What might help you be more confident that you are hearing from God? Ask God to reveal what would help you, and then write down what comes to mind. Test it to be sure it is consistent with the Bible, then practice that action.

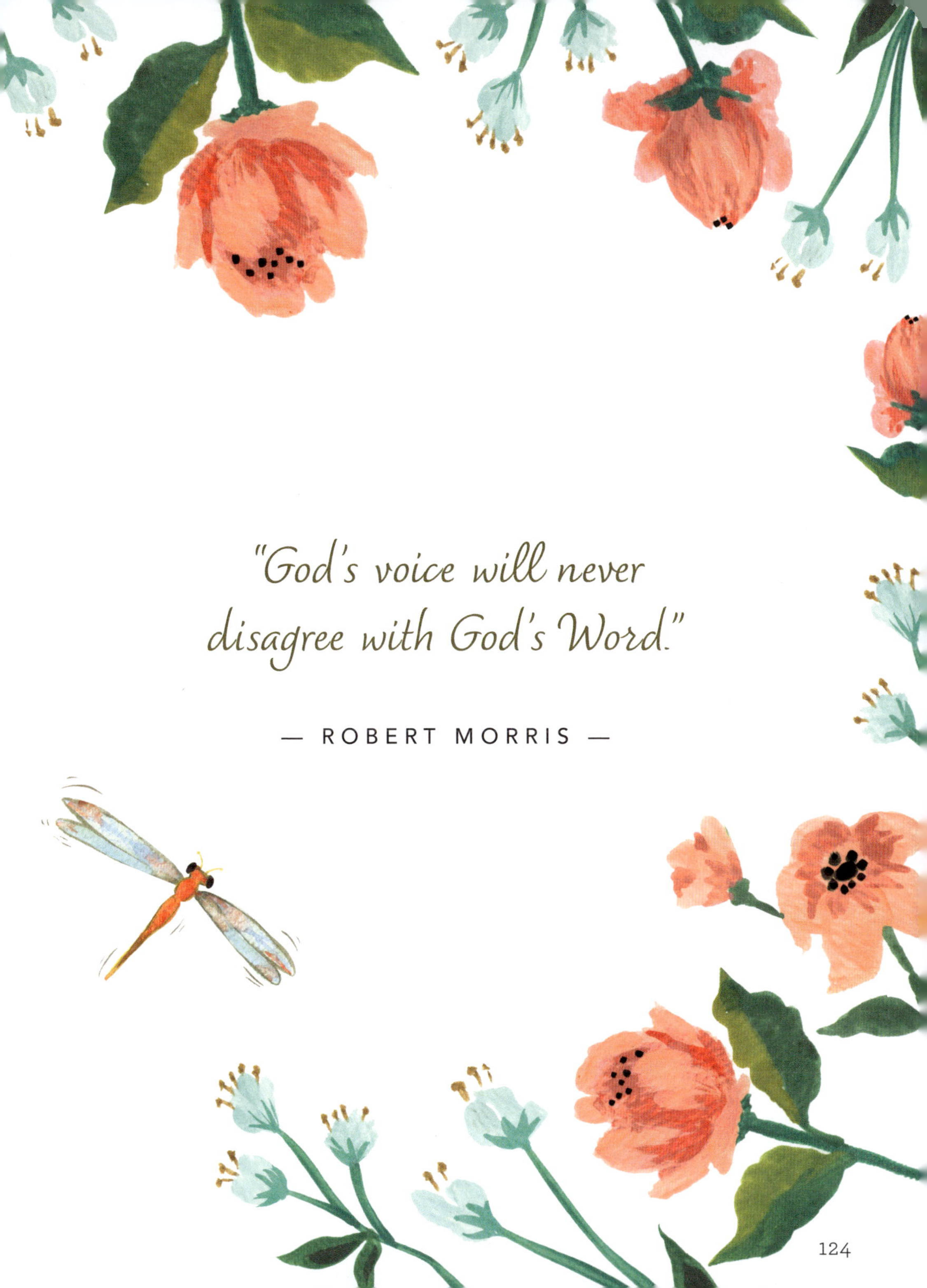

"God's voice will never disagree with God's Word."

— ROBERT MORRIS —

Day 32

Whatever you do, work at it with all your heart, as working for the Lord, not for human masters.

— COLOSSIANS 3:23

Hair on Fire

"Well, hello," said Melba in her Texas-Oklahoma twang. "I know I'm a little late in calling you back. I've been so busy!"

"Busy? What keeps a ninety-year-old so busy these days?" asked her son, Eric, while he glanced at his wife, who was chuckling in the background.

"Well," answered Melba, "I've been doing my church ministry every Friday, which is folding the bulletins, praying over all the seats of those God will be sending on Sunday, and then ministering to the pastoral team. And I've also had to drive some of my old friends to their doctor's appointments."

"Um, Mom? . . ." began Eric, winking at his wife. "How old are the old friends?" Eric's wife, Lisa, burst out laughing. Her mother-in-law, the revered matriarch of the Rice family, never ceased to amaze people with her attitude and energy. Her small Texas town's paper had just run a story on Melba, highlighting her twenty years with her pool aerobics club called "The Rusty Hinges." This group had worked out together three times a week for two decades and had all become fast friends.

But the true secret to Melba's rich life wasn't her activities; it was her joy in Jesus. She knew her God and communed with Him daily. Living in the same house for sixty years, situated on five acres of pecan trees, Melba would fling open her back door each morning and say, "Hello, world!" She fed the hummingbirds, then sat down with her Bible and communion elements, enjoying an hour conversing with her best friend, Jesus. She told everyone her hair was on fire for the Kingdom.

When asked how she was so sharp and happy and healthy, Melba responded, "Well, I've asked the Lord to take me as soon as I'm not useful to Him. When I can't help people anymore, then it will be my time to go."

Her time to go ended up being the age of ninety-five. Her funeral was filled with worship songs and happy stories about the far-reaching impact of one little woman.

What about you and me? What will our legacy be at the end of our days? I don't know about you, but I sure hope I age like Melba—full of selfless service, love, and life. I pray for that joy, such that aging will only be a state of mind and that I leave this earth with my hair on fire for the Kingdom.

Reflect

Most of us serve others in some way, but doing it joyfully is what pleases God and leaves a lasting legacy. In the verses preceding Philippians 2:3, we read about the sources of selflessness: "encouragement from being united with Christ . . . comfort from His love . . . sharing in the Spirit." What might you do to ensure you're receiving these from Christ daily so that your service to others is joyful? Write some suggestions below.

"Not all of us can do great things. But we can do small things with great love."

— MOTHER TERESA —

Day 33

Dear friends, don't be surprised at the fiery trials you are going through, as if something strange were happening to you. Instead, be very glad—for these trials make you partners with Christ in his suffering, so that you will have the wonderful joy of seeing his glory when it is revealed to all the world.

— 1 PETER 4:12

Know Who You Are

Research has found that what leads to most of our unhappiness is having unmet expectations. And I've come to realize that one of our most common, subconscious expectations is that because we are followers of God, we should be spared the trials of life.

But shouldn't we expect the opposite?

Over the years, I've had the chance to conduct several research interviews with military men in the world of special operations. They couldn't share details of the missions they had conducted behind enemy lines, so I didn't ask. But I did ask why. Why did they do what they did? Why were they willing to go into harm's way as regularly as the rest of us brave bad traffic jams?

I was struck by the theme that emerged: There's a higher purpose than just me. It's a dangerous world, with bad guys who will wreak havoc if someone doesn't do something about it. I can do something about it. In fact, I feel like I was built for this.

What I never heard was surprise. No one said, "I was so shocked to endure hardship when we were in the field." Even though many shared negative feelings of anger or grief, very few were disillusioned by it. They went into it *knowing* what awaited them.

Do we?

We don't think about it nearly often enough. But those of us who have given our lives to Christ are the spiritual equivalent of special forces agents. Except that instead of conducting missions into enemy territory, the Bible says we are living in it! (For example, 2 Corinthians 4:4 (NLT) describes Satan as "the god of this world.") We are end-times warriors, with a much higher purpose than just our daily lives: to work on behalf of another Kingdom and undermine the evil forces who are seeking to steal, kill, and destroy.

Yet our weapons are not the same as those of a Navy SEAL or an Army Ranger (2 Corinthians 10:4). Jesus instead says that since our battle isn't against flesh and blood, we must array ourselves "at all times" with His truth, righteousness, gospel, faith, salvation and Word (Ephesians 6:10-18). At all times. We have to live with this eternal mindset constantly, recognizing that we are special forces agents with a special calling, and that in the field we will have fiery trials. We will face persecution. And we should count it all joy because it is all part of a much, much greater ultimate purpose—something we were built for. And our trials here will seem so short and fleeting when compared to the delight of eternity.

Of course, our God says He wants wonderful things for us every day as well. Living with the knowledge that we will face trials in the field doesn't mean we miss out on delight. But it does mean we live, every day, knowing who we really are—and take great joy in it.

Reflect

What trials have you experienced? Are there ways that you have "partnered with Christ" through them? If so, note them below. If not, ask God to help you see how the trials are being used in your life—and how you are being used by Him!

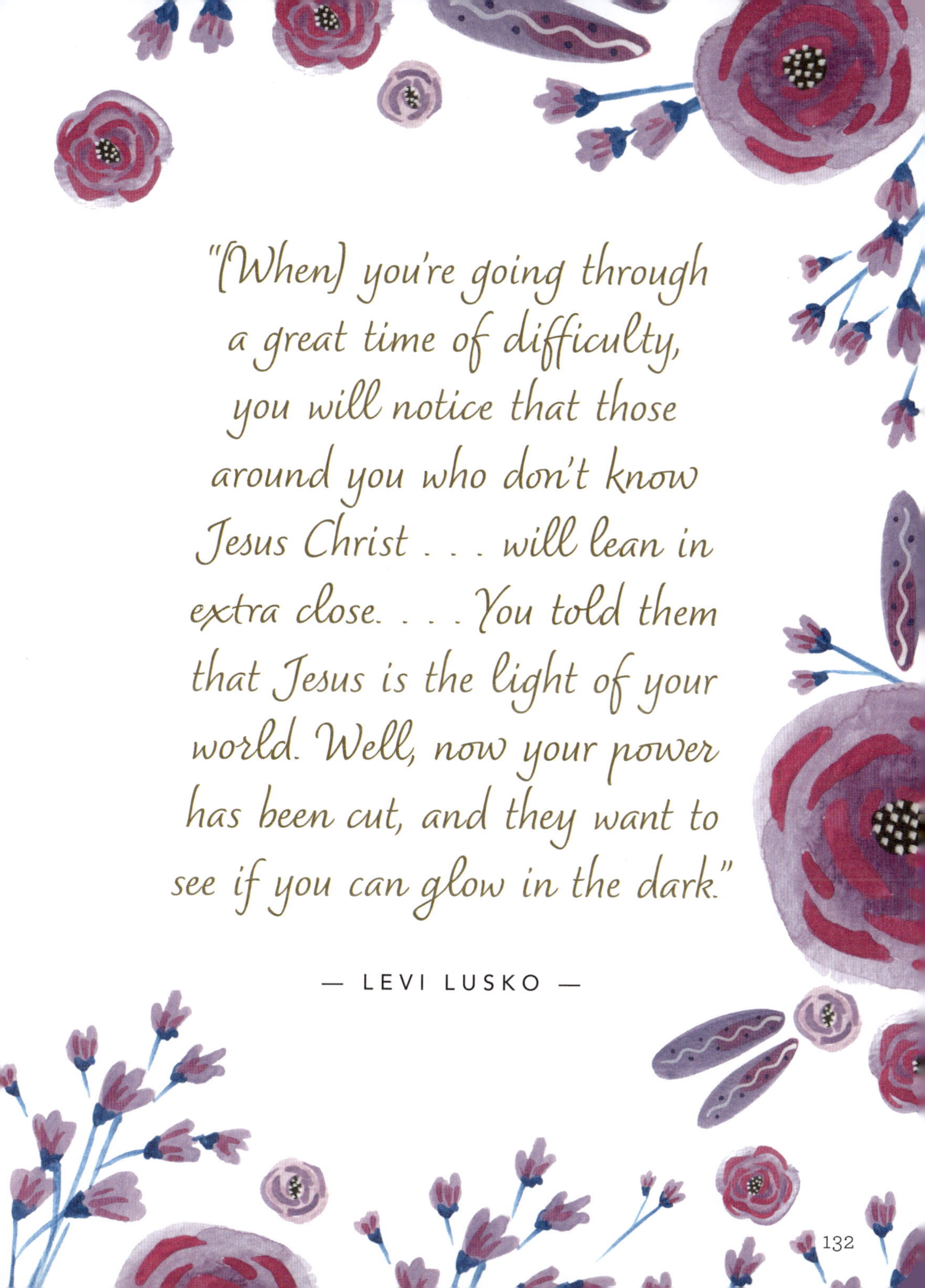

"[When] you're going through a great time of difficulty, you will notice that those around you who don't know Jesus Christ . . . will lean in extra close. . . . You told them that Jesus is the light of your world. Well, now your power has been cut, and they want to see if you can glow in the dark."

— LEVI LUSKO —

Day 34

Let me hear what God the Lord will speak,
for he will speak peace to his people, to his saints;
but let them not turn back to folly.

— PSALM 85:8, ESV

Honoring the Guardrails

When I was in high school, my family gathered all our frequent-flyer miles and took a camping trip in Europe. My parents were excited about a campground high in the Alps. But I was not so excited. I can still remember the hair-raising drive up the incredibly steep, narrow mountain road in our rental car. I was shocked to see that there were no guardrails. If our tires were off by just a foot, we would have gone over the edge. And it was easily a one-thousand-foot drop to the valley below. I remember saying, "Do they not care about the people who drive on this road?" I was upset!

When I got a little older and started hearing pastors preach on the importance of boundaries and guardrails, I made the connection—God has certain boundaries that He has put in place for our own good. They're His way of saying, "Don't go there or you're going to fall off a cliff! This guardrail is here for your protection. It's not there to hem you in or hold you back in a bad way, but in a good way—because I care about your well-being and because I love you."

If I'm in a situation where I am not finding joy, if I'm experiencing a great deal of stress in my life, one of the things I have to examine is this: Have I run past the guardrails that God has for my life? Because if I'm doing something that is actively disobedient to God or not in keeping with how He has designed me, how could a loving Father let me continue to live a life of great joy? It would be cruel to let me live happily in a way that was eventually going to destroy me.

Now, it is possible that we are honoring God's guardrails and our persistent stress is coming from somewhere else. But we always need to be willing to take an honest look at whether we are living in "folly"—in ways we know are unwise and wrong. And if we are, then we must be willing to repent, get back on the road, and reestablish honoring those guardrails.

Think about it: if there had been guardrails on that narrow mountain road in the Alps, I would have felt safe. I could have relaxed. And I would have felt free to fully enjoy the gorgeous scenery all around me. In the same way, the guardrails put in place by our loving heavenly Father keep us safe and set us free to find joy in the blessings and beauty that surround us every day as we walk with him. "You hem me in behind and before" (Psalm 139:5).

Reflect

Think about the guardrails that God leads us to place in our lives (sleep, prayer time, a budget, accountability . . .). Do you view those guardrails as more of a hindrance than a help? Have you been honoring them, or running straight through them as if they were not there? Privately, write down the important ways you may have been ignoring the guardrails. If you are willing, write a prayer of repentance, accept God's forgiveness, and commit to honoring those guardrails once again.

"Backsliding generally first begins with neglect of private prayer."

— J. C. RYLE —

Day 35

Rejoice always, pray continually, give thanks in all circumstances; for this is God's will for you in Christ Jesus.

— 1 THESSALONIANS 5:16-18

Botox for Your Brain

Your alarm didn't go off, you're out of coffee, and your sixth grader just told you that the materials for her exploding-volcano science project are due tomorrow. Before you know it, your eyes narrow, your face does that thing that lets your daughter know just how mad you are, and you give an exasperated sigh—at about the same time that you knock over the orange juice onto your purse.

If you're like me, this is about when you give out a frustrated scream and a few choice words that let everyone in the household know how not happy you are.

If you're like me, this is also (unfortunately) when you launch into your daughter for not telling you about the due date for the science materials. You ponder just letting her bear the consequences of not reminding you earlier, but then you decide to extend grace to her—although you do start scowling about all the supplies you're going to have to get.

Clearly, the volcano isn't the only thing that's close to exploding. You risk simmering and fuming all day.

What do you do when you are just irritated and having one of those days?

When I was writing The Kindness Challenge, I discovered masses of neuroscience research on how much our thoughts and body language direct our feelings. Here was my favorite one: In 2008, British researchers investigated reports by plastic surgeons wondering whether Botox, in addition to reducing wrinkles, might also be an antidepressant. After the patients had Botox injections, many of these women and men reported feeling more positive about life. The researchers discovered it wasn't an antidepressant at all: instead, Botox paralyzes the frown muscles. And when these people couldn't frown or scowl, they simply felt less, well, "frowny." They couldn't maintain those negative feelings and found the positive feelings coming much more naturally![11]

One of my favorite verses in the Bible is Philippians 4:8 (NLT), where we're instructed to "Rejoice!" by doing this: "fix your thoughts on what is true, and honorable, and right, and pure, and lovely, and admirable. Think about things that are excellent and worthy of praise." In other words: try to stop yourself from simmering about all the very real irritating (frowny) stuff and think about the very real positives. Yes, you're late for work, you've got an orange-juice-sticky purse, and you'll need to somehow leave work early to get the science project materials. But you know what? You've got a job that helps to pay the bills. And far more important, you have an amazing daughter, who is healthy and who loves you.

If you spend the drive to work thinking about *that,* and even force a smile onto your face, it's like Botox for your mind and heart. You will find much of your irritation simply melting away.

Sisters, when we're irritated, let's skip the Botox shots and just remember to think on whatever is lovely!

Reflect

What has been bothering you lately? In Philippians 4, God kindly follows the command to "rejoice in the Lord always" with practical steps: first, pray your requests to God with thanksgiving ("Lord, will you help? I'm late and irritated! But thank You for my children and Your provision"); then, refocus to "whatever is lovely." Use this model to write a prayer below about that thing that's been bothering you—and thanking God for something about it.

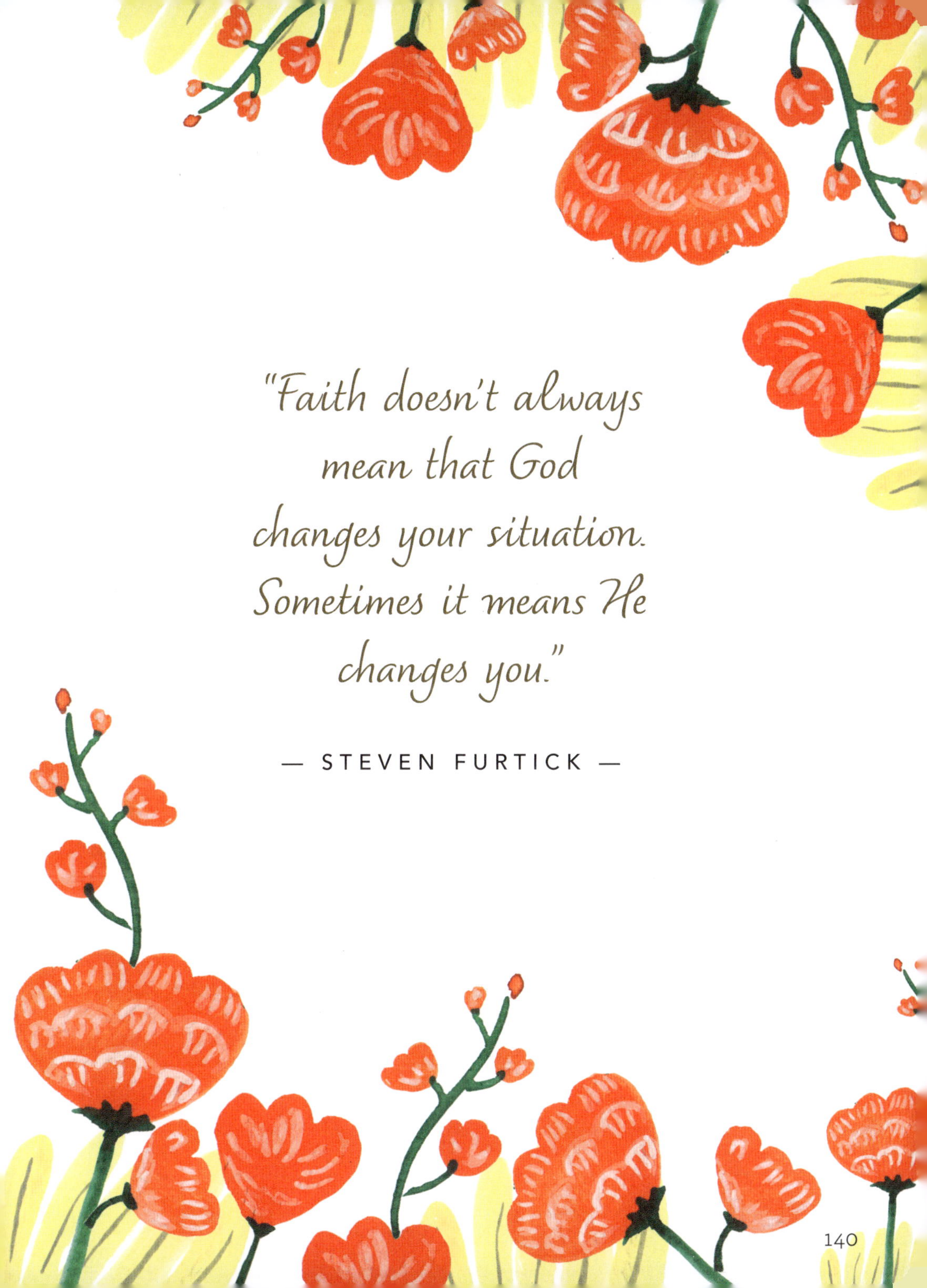

"Faith doesn't always mean that God changes your situation. Sometimes it means He changes you."

— STEVEN FURTICK —

Day 36

Be kind to one another, tenderhearted, forgiving one another, as God in Christ forgave you.

— EPHESIANS 4:32, ESV

The Stolen Screenplay

"I'm so excited!" said my friend. "I can't wait to see what comes of this."

My friend Jana and her husband had spent years as independent screenwriters and filmmakers. But they felt called to more; they wanted to be involved in a mainstream movie. One day Jana felt God strongly directing her to write a script about the fascinating life story of an important historical figure.

After months of research, writing, and prayer, an influential Christian couple—well-known Hollywood producers—asked to see the screenplay.

As Jana sent it off, she was realistic (very few screenplays actually become movies) but still thrilled by their interest and eager for feedback. Each time she called the producers for updates, they assured her they were looking at it, but were just busy. They did have a few notes. Once things slowed down, they would provide input.

Then they stopped returning calls.

Months later, Jana learned the Hollywood couple had a film in the works . . . and it was very similar to the story she had sent. Beating all the odds, the movie actually went into production. A year later, the movie was released and became a success at the box office.

Jana and her husband were in turmoil. They fought anger and bitterness at this apparent betrayal. And not by a random competitor, but by trusted Christians!

They knew they couldn't give in to anger, but they also didn't know where to put their raging emotions. That's when they realized they were being asked to step into a higher level of faith. In this life, *every* Christian walks through the valley of betrayal. The enemy *always* wants to dangle the bait of bitterness. Would they give in to the temptation to grab it? Or would they do the one thing that would free their hearts?

Choosing to *truly* forgive someone who has devastated us is one of the hardest things we can ever do. Yet it is the only path to having our joy restored. It also brings us to an entirely new level of maturity in God's Kingdom. We all want to be found faithful . . . but the path to get there goes through the profound choice to forgive. And it doesn't stop there. It often means going further and *blessing* the person who has wronged us.

Jana and her husband got on their knees and asked God's blessing over the producers and the movie. They thanked God for advancing His Kingdom through their project—even without being given the credit or involvement their hearts desired. And as freedom and gladness rose up in them, they realized they were being given something far more important.

Reflect

Do you have anyone you view as a "competitor" in some way? Someone you're jealous of, or who perhaps has been unfair to you? Now, remember that God asks us, "Bless those who persecute you. Don't curse them; pray that God will bless them." Write below a prayer, sincerely asking God to bless this person. Now consider: what does that do in your heart?

"To be wronged is nothing, unless you continue to remember it."

— CONFUCIUS —

Day 37

So if you sinful people know how to give good gifts to your children, how much more will your heavenly Father give good gifts to those who ask him.

— MATTHEW 7:11, NLT

He Wants Our Good

In the 1890s, with the explosion in manufacturing, tenement apartment buildings were erected in New York City. The quickly-constructed apartments all had the same floor plan, with each tenant's bedroom above the one below. Since the floors and walls were thin and everyone worked different shifts, a new type of dread entered the lexicon: Waiting for the other shoe to drop.

In the middle of the night, if a resident was asleep, they could easily be awakened by the sounds from the apartment above them, especially if it was a workman coming home from a late-night shift. The frustrated resident would listen, staring at the ceiling, as their neighbor clumped into his bedroom and removed one heavy shoe at a time. There would be a loud thunk as the first shoe hit the floor, and the sleepy resident would wait, teeth on edge, for the next one.

"Waiting for the other shoe to drop" is a colloquial expression that has come to mean expecting and waiting for the something bad that is sure to happen.

It also so often captures how we feel about our life with God. We see the blessings. But part of us, subconsciously, is waiting for the bad thing that is sure to come.

We watch miraculous things happen, but we don't let ourselves get too excited about them. After all, Jesus said, "In this world you will have trouble" (John 16:33), right?

Subconsciously, we look at the college we're amazed we got into, the job we enjoy going to, the amazing spouse, or the home God provided for our family . . . and we wonder when it is all going to fall to pieces around us.

Two thousand years ago, Jesus looked at people just like us and said, essentially, "There's no reason the next thing along will be bad. God adores you. You need to let yourself believe that God wants wonderful things for your life!"

Sisters, it is very hard to live a life of joy while expecting the other shoe to drop. Yes, of course in this world we will have trouble. But as Jesus said over and over, our God loves us even more than we love our own children. If we who are imperfect people want great things for our kids, how much more does our perfect heavenly Father want to see us not just survive, but thrive?

Oh we of little faith! Instead of believing in (having faith in) the bad things of this world, let's believe in our amazing, wonderful, loving Abba Father. When Jesus called God "Abba," he was using the tender term, "Daddy." Whether or not our own earthly father was an unconditionally loving, tender "Daddy" or not, we can look at all the good things God has given us and realize: our heavenly Father is.

Reflect

Do you find yourself waiting for the other shoe to drop? If you have trouble trusting that God truly wants good things for you, why is that? Because He sometimes lets bad things happen, too? Because you think you don't deserve it? Write your reasons below. Then ask yourself, how do you think God wants you to respond to those reasons? Write a prayer to God, asking Him to help you see and believe in His good intentions toward you.

"If we knew what God knows, we would ask exactly for what He gives."

— TIM KELLER —

Day 38

Whatever you do, do it all for the glory of God.

— 1 CORINTHIANS 10:31

Whatever

I was boarding an airplane on the way to a speaking event when the cheery flight attendant at the door pointed to my necklace and started to chuckle. "Whatever!" he said, holding up his hands in a "W" and referencing the word that hung from my neck. "That's so true. Whatever, right?!"

People were lined up behind me, pushing me forward, so I just laughed and kept moving. My necklace did, in fact, say "Whatever," and it's one of my favorite pieces of jewelry. But not because of how our culture cynically says "It doesn't matter. . . . Whatever." It actually refers to some of my favorite verses in the Bible—the "whatevers." The instruction to think about "Whatever is true, whatever is noble, whatever is right . . ." (Philippians 4:8) The commitment that "Whatever you have commanded us we will do, and wherever you send us we will go" (Joshua 1:16). And many others, including today's verse: "Whatever you do, do it all for the glory of God."

Which is why, as I made my way down the aisle, I didn't feel joyful. I felt convicted. I had a brief moment where I could've shown God glory with a few words to the flight attendant about what my necklace meant. Not cultural cynicism or indifference, but something beautiful and eternal that he may have needed.

First Peter 3:15 (NET) asks us to "always be ready to give an answer to anyone who asks about the hope you possess." In the ten seconds it took to shuffle by that man, I could've smiled and said, "It's actually from verses in the Bible that start with 'Whatever.' It reminds me to focus on *whatever* is good and lovely and true, or that God hears us, *whatever* we ask (1 John 5:15), or that *whatever* I do, I'm supposed to be pointing people to Him."

There will always be more joy in our lives when we glorify our Father. He wants us to share the hope we've been given, the love we've received, and the blessings that have been bestowed upon us. It can be as simple as making eye contact with a stranger and smiling. Or as involved as listening to God's nudge to offer to pray for someone who looks like they need it.

I decided from that point on to have something on hand to say the next time someone commented on my necklace. Or if I was asked where I was headed on my ministry trip. Or if someone mentioned the cross on my bracelet.

God doesn't necessarily need us to speak a sermon into a stranger's ear, but He does want us sharing His love.

Reflect

Do you have a Christian T-shirt, necklace, bag, or some other article that people might ask about? Picture a stranger in the grocery store saying, "What does that mean?" How would you answer? Write a simple statement below of what you might say, and maybe even practice it so that if you are asked for an answer for the hope that is within you, you will have a starting point for what you might say.

"I give all the glory to God. It's kind of a win-win situation. The glory goes up to Him and the blessings fall down on me."

— GABBY DOUGLAS —

[Mary] sat at the Lord's feet, listening to what [Jesus] taught. But Martha . . . said, "Lord, doesn't it seem unfair to you that my sister just sits here while I do all the work? Tell her to come and help me." But the Lord said to her, "My dear Martha, you are worried and upset over all these details! There is only one thing worth being concerned about. Mary has discovered it, and it will not be taken away from her."

— LUKE 10:39-42, NLT

Paying Attention

"I know God loves us," said Camila to her friend Sarah as she glanced at her GPS, "but why doesn't He speak to us? With everything going on in my life, I *need* to hear from Him."

Sarah somehow maintained a sense of joy and direction from the Lord even in the midst of the greatest storms. Now that Camila was facing her own storms, she wanted Sarah's secret.

Sarah paused. Finally, she said, "He *does* speak. I'll tell you how to hear from Him, but I promise you won't like the answer."

"Tell me anyway," Camila replied, as she drove through the crowded streets.

"You have to turn off the flow of everything that is distracting you right now. Turn off social media. Stop the flow of the news. Set your alarm, wake up early, and have coffee with the Lord."

Ugh. Sarah was right. This definitely wasn't what Camila wanted to hear. Social media was Camila's constant connection to the world. If she turned it off, her friends would be upset. How would she keep up with her sorority sisters? If she turned off the news, how would she know what was happening in politics?

Sarah knew exactly what she was thinking. She smiled ruefully. "How much do you *really* want to hear from God? Do you want the true God who is your Master, but also your friend? Or do you secretly want the magic genie in the sky who downloads His directions at your request? That's not Him. If you want to hear from your boss, or from a friend, you have to cut out all distractions and pay attention to that person. You wouldn't surf social media while your boss is talking to you, or at lunch with a friend. It would be rude, and you wouldn't hear them properly. It's the same thing with God. You have to cut out whatever keeps you from hearing that still, small voice."

Camilla was convicted. How many conversations had she missed with the Lord because of the distractions she allowed to consume her days?

What about you? Can you relate to the excuses Camila came up with to justify her cluttered life? I know I can. Or, do you ever secretly want directions from God without the investment of time in your relationship with Him? Oh, that is so convicting! How willing are we to turn off *anything* that keeps us from hearing Him?

In His presence there is *fullness* of joy. There is no distraction, no momentary hit of interest from the latest news or the latest update video, that is worth missing *HIM.*

Reflect

What are some ways you can be sure to spend time with the Lord on a daily basis? When you become distracted, what are some ways you can get back on course? Write those down and practice them for the next few weeks.

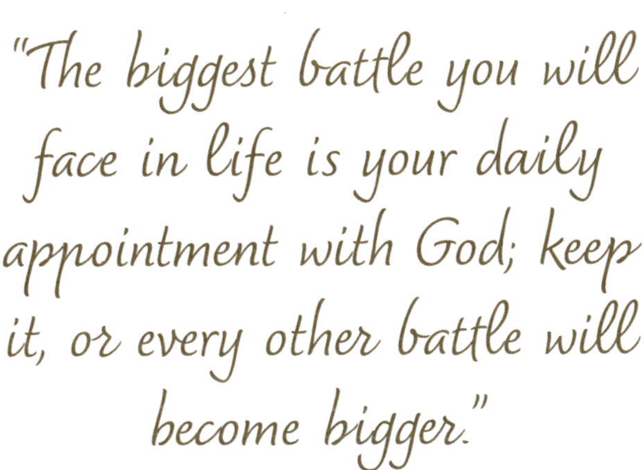

"The biggest battle you will face in life is your daily appointment with God; keep it, or every other battle will become bigger."

— RAVI ZACHARIAS —

Day 40

Be strong and courageous. Do not be afraid or terrified because of them, for the Lord your God goes with you; he will never leave you nor forsake you.

— DEUTERONOMY 31:6

A Path through the Panic

"I'm scared!" Cherice listened in horror as her seventeen-year-old niece, Abby, described an outbreak of strange, violent behavior from her dad. He was Cherice's only sibling, Abby's mom had died years before, and they lived several states apart. Cherice urged her to race to a friend's house where she could be safe.

Cherice tried to speak with her brother, but something was very wrong. She learned later that he had experienced a stroke in the brain region that governed impulses and erratic behavior.

Cherice was scared and unsure what to do. She shot up almost incoherent prayers as she tried to figure out police, court, and safe-haven interventions.

Anyone who has ever been in a panicky place can probably relate. When the scary situation is all we can see, it is hard to think straight, much less turn to God for a coherent planning session. Yet, that is exactly when we need to turn to God—trusting that He is in control and has a path for us through the panic.

Remember

As Cherice prayed, a biblical story kept coming to mind, that of God protecting the terrified Israelites who were fleeing Egypt, then making a clear path through the Red Sea. Even after the immediate trauma, when they had no idea what to do, God guided their steps with pillars of fire and cloud.

"Lord," Cherice prayed, "I may not be a pillar of fire, but I need something to show our path!"

Within days, she noticed connections happening that could only be from God. A local family offered a safe place for Abby. Caring officials arranged for her to finish her senior year at her original school. And the same police officer who just "happened" to be specially trained to deal with mental instability also just "happened" to be on duty whenever there was a need. What gifts!

Then the officer advised Cherice to involuntarily commit her brother. As she stood before the judge, she felt that turmoil rising again—the turmoil many of us feel even after so many miraculous signposts. *Was this the right thing?* As the judge granted her request, he told Cherice, "Thank you for your courage to do this. Are you familiar with Esther in the Bible? She risked her life to save others."

It was as if God had audibly said, "You see? I'm still leading. Trust me."

A year later, with her brother in recovery and her niece reconciled to him, Cherice says, "Those events had to be from God. There was no other explanation. So now when I face fear, I don't just remember the Israelites: I remember last year. It reminds me that *He is faithful.*" Sisters, peace doesn't come from having the path figured out, peace comes when we remember that we are holding the hand of the One who does.

Reflect

Think of a time or two in which you were very uncertain and worried. Recall how you saw God work in the situation and how the experience affected your faith. Finally, ask the most crucial question: have you allowed that experience to continue to affect your faith? What can you do to keep the fire of faith burning?

"Remembering the specific ways [God has] been faithful in the past trains us to look for evidences of His goodness, might, faithfulness, love, mercy and protection in the future. Don't forget to remember."

— WHITNEY CAPPS —

He guides the humble in what is right and teaches them his way. All the ways of the Lord are loving and faithful toward those who keep the demands of his covenant.

— PSALM 25: 9-10

Feet Washed, Heart Refreshed

It had been a rough summer, and Nina's nerves were raw. With six children out of school for the summer, she was already stretched. Then her seven-year-old son, Adam, got the worst case of swimmer's ear her doctor had ever seen.

Gone were his fun days at the pool, swim team, and water park. Yet Nina had five other kids, and the pool was their main inexpensive activity, so Adam still had to go . . . but he just sat in the hot, muggy shade and stewed.

Nina knew his little spirit was broken, and she tried to arrange non-water-related fun over the next three weeks, but it didn't change much. If he was a cartoon character, he would've had a big, ugly cloud over his head and steam coming out of his (wounded) ears. His grumpiness was making life miserable for everyone.

In these situations, we can love the person who is making our life miserable and still feel our own low-grade annoyance or resentment stewing, can't we? Nina prayed for God to change her heart.

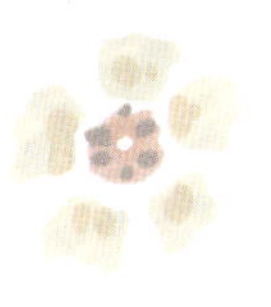

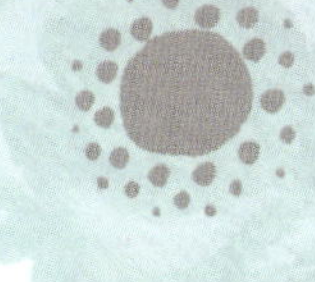
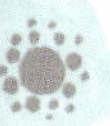

One morning Nina was cleaning the bathroom when Adam wandered in. "Could you rub my feet?" he asked. On her knees, toilet brush in hand, she gave Adam a look that said, "you can't be serious!" Nina told him she was a little, uh, busy right now. He nodded and wandered away and was as grumpy as usual at the pool that day.

That evening, she was in the kitchen making dinner when Adam wandered in again. "Can you rub my feet now?"

Nina wanted to sigh and say, "How about you rub MY feet?! I'm the one who's been doing chores, watching six children at the pool, and managing your attitude!" But instantly, this thought arrived: *Rub his feet. He's hurting, and he needs you.* She felt like God was saying, *Do this because I've asked you to.*

She got some nice-smelling lotion, put it on her hands, and spent a few minutes rubbing his feet. And as she saw Adam relax, she suddenly felt something relax in her own tense, stressed-out heart. Instead of the annoyance she'd been feeling toward Adam, she realized she felt love. Compassion. A sweetness was rising in her heart that had been sorely lacking the last few weeks.

It was a sweetness she had prayed for, and it came because she had served her little wounded boy in a way that connected with his heart.

Nina realized: although she had been *doing* a lot for Adam over the last few weeks, she hadn't really been *serving* him. She'd been trying to manage him.

God's ways are miraculous. A true moment of service that touches someone else's heart can refresh ours.

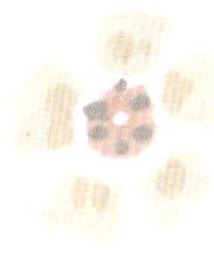

Reflect

Have you had a low-grade annoyance with someone recently? Several someones? Take a moment to list those people. Next to each of their names, write a simple way you could serve them in a way that matters to that person and will connect with their heart. Now, pray: which person and action does God want you to pick? Do that action this week, and come back and record what happens.

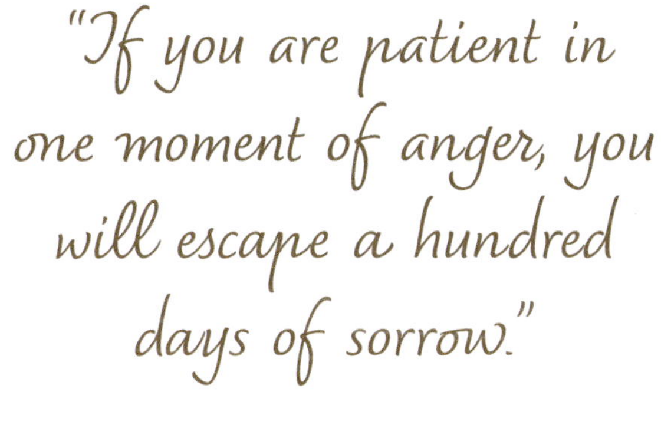

"If you are patient in one moment of anger, you will escape a hundred days of sorrow."

— CHINESE PROVERB —

Day 42

So if the Son sets you free, you will be free indeed.

— JOHN 8:36

Free Indeed

A woman I'll call Mia was wrongfully accused of a crime, sent to prison, and wasn't sure if the truth would ever be known. She was increasingly angry and bitter. Even if eventually released, nothing would give her back the time she had lost. And it was a cold and difficult place to endure.

One particular day, the women were allowed out in the prison yard. They were able to get some sunshine and fresh air and see a little grass. But Mia didn't see the sunshine. Anger churned in her heart as she walked the walls with her new cellmate, a twenty-four-year-old woman who had small children back at home. Mia was overcome with the usual feelings of injustice. She angrily said, "Even when we're outside, we aren't free. We're surrounded by barbed wire; everything reminds us of our imprisonment. I feel like a caged bird." Her cellmate grinned, threw out her arms, and lifted her face to the sun, her eyes closed. "I'm free," she said.

Mia was confused. "What do you mean?"

Her new friend smiled, "I'm free to worship Jesus." She pressed her hand against her chest. "I'm free in *here*."

This young woman explained that when she gave her life to Jesus, she suddenly experienced an incredible *lightness* for the first time in her life. God had miraculously lifted her bondage to sin, to always looking for the next con, to a life of self-focus. Suddenly she wanted to live for Him. She knew this was her time to be a light in a dark place—to be an example to her children of grace in difficulty. Imprisoned and surrounded by barbed wire, she was freer than any woman living without Christ on the outside.

Mia had known Jesus from her early years. And yet she suddenly saw herself as she was: held captive by anger and bitterness far more than by the walls around her. Yes, she was experiencing dreadful injustice. But couldn't God use this situation she found herself in? Was this life really about her?

She began to think spiritually instead of physically about her circumstances. Surely her great God was in control, which meant He had plans for her even here. And if she was free in the most important ways that matter, of *course* she could have joy!

Can't we do the same? We all have situations that make us feel trapped. Maybe it's a feeling of helplessness about not having the marriage, child, or degree we wanted. Maybe it's being chronically underemployed, or an addiction or mental illness with seemingly no way of escape. But our God has set us free *in our hearts!* What an awesome God to give us the ability to experience freedom and joy no matter what.

Reflect

What is your barbed-wired fence right now—that thing that is making you feel trapped? What difference does it make to realize that because of Jesus' saving grace, you can have freedom in your heart, regardless of your circumstances? Write a prayer to God thanking Him for your salvation and your ability to rise above your difficulties in that area.

"I have heard of some good old woman in a cottage, who had nothing but a piece of bread and a little water. Lifting up her hands, she said as a blessing, 'What! All this, and Christ too?'"

— CHARLES SPURGEON —

Day 43

The Lord is my shepherd, I have all that I need.

— PSALM 23:1, NLT

Trusting the *Real* Shepherd

Sheep are scarce in Atlanta. I'm close to busy interstates, malls, and parks, but no sheep-filled pastures. In fact, when our family drives into a rural area, it's not long before someone yells from the back seat, "Look, cows! Sheep!"

Although my life is far removed from that of a shepherd, I can imagine the responsibilities involved. Among the rocky hills in the wilderness, a good shepherd lives daily with his flock, knowing each by name. He keeps his sheep from dangerous predators and thorny thickets. He leads his sheep to food and water. He tends carefully to those who are sick or injured.

If God is our shepherd, we should always be content to stay by Him, never wandering away to other shepherds. Right?

Three years ago, my friend's husband applied for a well-paying job in a picturesque mountain town. Lydia was thrilled to discover he was in the top five finalists out of 100 candidates. Her heart became attached. Not only was this a promotion, it was in their dream location. She believed it was the perfect move for their family, the perfect job for her husband.

She told me later, though, that she could almost hear her heart whisper, "This job is my shepherd, I have all that I need." Her trust had subtly shifted to a lesser shepherd.

How often do we take something besides God and try to make it our true shepherd? If we struggle with our health, we think, "This new doctor is my shepherd." If we struggle with our children, we think, "Finding the right school is my shepherd." If we struggle with self-confidence, we think, "Losing twenty pounds is my shepherd." Although health, parenting, and self-improvement are not bad goals, they make terrible shepherds. Earthly masters cater to what we want, but they can never know what we truly need.

Guess what? Lydia's husband didn't get that perfect job. Instead, God, their *true* Good Shepherd, moved them in the opposite direction. Much to her surprise, the move has been a blessing—full of rich opportunities, life-giving relationships, and a path to knowing Him more deeply.

Oh, the riches of recognizing that our Good Shepherd knows what we need, and He gives us exactly that.

Reflect

What "lesser shepherds" do you tend to stray toward? These are the things, people, or experiences that you may not have right now, and are wishing for, thinking, "Things would be better if ____." Knowing that your True Shepherd knows and supplies all your needs, consider: why might He be delaying or denying any of those things you haven't yet seen come to fruition? Thank Him for watching over you so tenderly.

"Sometimes you are delayed where you are because God knows there's a storm where you're headed."

— AUTHOR UNKNOWN —

Day 44

A man has joy by the answer of his mouth,
And a word spoken in due season, how good it is!

— PROVERBS 15:23, NKJV

The Uncomfortable Rule

In every study about the causes of happiness, peace, health, and wellness, strong relationships top the list. . . . And in every study about the causes of stress, depression, and discouragement, loneliness or relationship troubles top the list.

God has wired us for relationship. One of His greatest gifts is for us to live in fellowship with others. So one of His great commands is to do everything we can to make that fellowship good. To live at peace with all men. To give and receive. To build one another up. To accept rebukes gracefully. To give a word in season, when it is needed.

Yet that last one is sometimes an obstacle, isn't it? A word spoken in season implies that a word is needed. Which means, among other things, that if there's an issue that could cause problems in the relationship, we are supposed to bring it up.

Eek.

No passive-aggressive holding back. *My roommate, my spouse, my friend should know what bothers me. And if they don't, then I'm not going to tell them.*

No skulking in self-pity. *They don't care that I'm the one always cleaning up after them.*

No assuming the worst. *I can't believe they went to the movie without me. They are trying to exclude me.*

Instead: God asks us to speak a word in season. ("You're so much fun, and I love sharing the apartment with you. But I don't think you realize how much work it puts on my shoulders when you leave your dishes for me to clean.") Yes, having grace is vitally important, too. And constantly cataloguing problems is damaging. But if there is an issue that the other person would want to know about and which would otherwise bother you over the long term, stuffing down an issue isn't having grace. It is setting yourself up to live in unforgiveness.

One of the wisest pieces of advice I've seen for relationships actually comes from a book for college students. In *The Naked Roommate,* author Harlan Cohen suggests that roommates mutually adopt what he calls the Uncomfortable Rule: If your roommate is doing something that makes you uncomfortable, you must raise it within 24–48 hours. If you don't, then you're saying that what they are doing is fine with you, and you can't bring it up ever again.[12]

We would do well to adopt this principle for our close relationships. Let's give ourselves and those we love the joy of true fellowship. Yes, we will still have to offer grace when the other person finds it hard to make a change. And we will sometimes still need to offer forgiveness. But speaking a word in season, in love, may mean we never get to the point of broken relationships and the need for forgiveness in the first place.

Reflect

Are you struggling not to resent someone? Read Proverbs 15:23 again. The phrase "in due season" is also translated "timely." Waiting to confront someone breeds resentment. How can you have a "timely" conversation with that person, where you wait long enough to be calm and gentle, but have the conversation soon enough to avert resentment? Ask God to show you if and when you should confront this person, then write out what you might say below. Conclude with a prayer for the ability to "speak the truth in love" (see Ephesians 4:15).

"Speak in such a way that
others love to listen to you.
Listen in such a way that
others love to speak to you."

— ANONYMOUS —

Day 45

Rejoice with those who rejoice;
mourn with those who mourn.

— ROMANS 12:15

Prayers on the Walls

The community was shocked. We had just learned that a local Christian husband and father of several school-age children had taken his own life. The heartbroken friends of the family felt helpless to know what to do to love them through it. Many were hesitant, wanting to "give them space." Many others worried about saying the wrong thing to the grieving widow and children.

It's easy to rejoice with those who rejoice, isn't it? When it is a wedding, new baby, or promotion, we easily enter into our friends' joy. But God also calls us to mourn with others when the time comes. That is so much harder. It takes strength not to pull back, and instead look into a friend's deep pain and say, "I'll join you where you are. I will walk with you through this."

A group of friends did that for this grieving, shocked family. Meals were arranged, prayer chains were set up, and a steady stream of people offered them support. But the reality was, something terrible had happened in their home office, and they couldn't bear to look at the room.

So with the widow's blessing, this group of friends made a plan.

Over the course of an afternoon when she and the kids were gone, the friends would empty the room, paint the walls, bring in new furniture, and create a totally different look for the space.

But what they did first took my breath away.

Before they started painting, each friend took a pencil and started writing prayers that covered the walls. Tears streamed down their faces as they mourned for their friend and her children. They wrote Scripture and prayers and promises and praises until the walls were completely covered.

When they painted over them, they felt as if they were sealing in the prayers, surrounding the family with hundreds of faithful petitions on their behalf.

And when the family saw the room, a terrible weight lifted. One of the children, a freshman in high school, said she could tangibly feel the presence and comfort of Jesus there. She said she knew she would want to spend a lot of time in that room.

In a time of great sorrow or hardship, serving others is such an important bridge to the inexplicable, profound "joy of the Lord" that does not change with circumstances. The friends' tangible help was crucial. But their emotional and spiritual help was priceless. And what deep tenderness these women found as they rallied around their mourning friends and saw *them* entering into God's joy.

Reflect

Second Corinthians 1:3-4 calls God, "the Father of compassion and God of all comfort, who comforts us in all our troubles, so that we can comfort those in any trouble." What are some ways that you can show comfort to someone who is hurting? When the time comes, how can you ensure that you follow through on your intention to comfort? Write these down so that when needed, you can put your plans into action. If you know of someone who needs comforting now, make a plan for helping them.

"God does not comfort us to make us comfortable, but to make us comforters."

— JOHN HENRY JOWETT —

Day 46

Human anger does not produce the righteousness God desires.

— JAMES 1:20, NLT

Don't Vent Away Your Joy

When Anika and Kevin adopted a young boy who had been traumatized from birth, they quickly learned that he had a lot of rage, anger, and sadness—and it was daily going to be heaped onto his new mom.

Thankfully, Anika found a support group of similar moms that met every week or so. Suddenly, sanity! These women *intimately* understood her journey and could help navigate the choppy waters. For several years they shared stories, tears, groans, laughter, advice—and supported each other in hardships that would be difficult for an "outsider" to comprehend.

One day, when her son was seven years old, Anika heard about an initiative I had developed called The 30-day Kindness Challenge,[13] which helps improve your relationship with any person in your life. She instinctively felt God calling her to do it for her son. But she was a bit panicked about one of the main requirements: for 30 days, you say *nothing negative* about your person—either *to* them or *about* them to someone else! What about her support group? How would it work if she couldn't say anything negative about her son and their struggles?

Despite her misgivings, she went ahead with the challenge . . . and had a deep, convicting realization at the next support group meeting.

Anika realized that talking negatively about the experiences with her son had not actually been as healthy or as helpful as she originally thought. Instead, she had been feeling . . . pleasure. She hadn't been bringing forward these stories to get sober-minded advice and prayer as much as for the pleasure of saying, "You would not *believe* what happened yesterday!"

She had been using that time with her friends to express her own anger and stoke the fire of discontent, and—if she was truly honest with herself—a deep worry that things would never change.

When we're angry, we think it is healthy to vent or "let out a little steam" from the kettle so it doesn't explode, right?

Wrong. Neuroscientists have found the truth is the opposite. When we "vent" in that way, we are actually *activating* an interconnected anger system in the brain. We're actually turning *up* the heat![14]

Sisters, ironically, when we "vent," it isn't the bad feelings that are leaving us. It is our joy.

Anika realized she did indeed need to share about certain difficulties with her son. But when she reported it neutrally, as if she were sharing a news article, she eliminated the angry pleasure she had been feeling. She found herself genuinely seeking advice and also feeling less angry toward her son. A surprising, sweet joy began filling her heart. She really did love her son. And for the first time in a long time, she felt hopeful that things could change for the better.

Reflect

What are the places and situations in which you tend to vent, roll your eyes, or share negative thoughts with others? Write those below. Then pray over each one and ask for God's help to focus on honoring Him in those situations instead. Next to each situation, write an alternative way of handling it or how you can turn the situation to be a more healthy, positive, encouraging one.

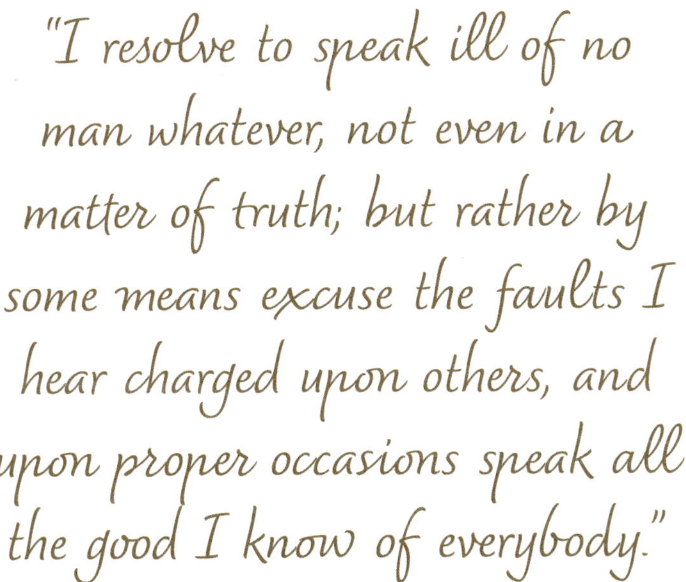

"I resolve to speak ill of no man whatever, not even in a matter of truth; but rather by some means excuse the faults I hear charged upon others, and upon proper occasions speak all the good I know of everybody."

— BENJAMIN FRANKLIN —

Day 47

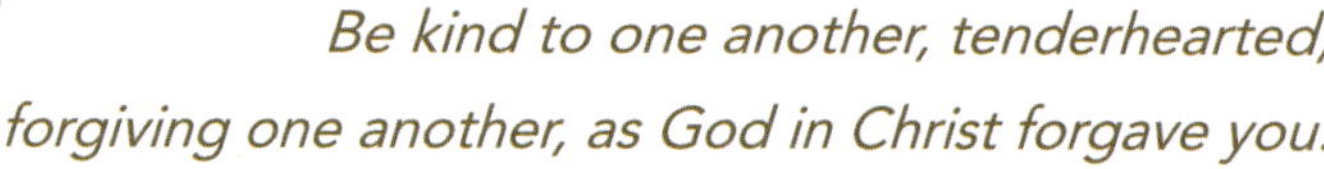
*Be kind to one another, tenderhearted,
forgiving one another, as God in Christ forgave you.*

— EPHESIANS 4:32, ESV

When It's Your Child Who's Hurt

When my daughter Morgen started a new elementary school, she instantly attracted the attention of a classmate—and not in a good way. This girl commanded the loyalty of the girls in class and apparently decided my shy daughter was a perfect target to be bullied.

Every day, Morgen came home crying about both the bullying and having no friends. Girls in the class liked her, but the bully wouldn't "allow" them to befriend her. Several times the bully included Morgen in things, only to demand rule-breaking that Morgen was uncomfortable with. Which only made the rift wider.

We addressed it with the parents and school. We tried to help Morgen with boundaries and give her strategies. We explained that bullying came from deep insecurity. We tried to help her ignore it and hold her head high. All our approaches had limited success.

It was excruciating for our sweet daughter and for us. What could we do? Should we switch schools? Keep getting angry and upset when Morgen dissolved into tears? Keep praying for the bully, while seething inside?

In these pages, we've been talking about the importance of forgiveness to heart freedom. But if you're like me, it's a lot harder to forgive someone who hurts your child!

It seemed crazy that this young girl had such power to make our lives miserable.

We finally realized we couldn't restore joy to our lives unless something changed. Meaning *we had to change.*

Since we didn't want to leave the school, we had to teach Morgen (and ourselves) how to forgive someone even when they do not repent or ask for forgiveness.

Friends, sometimes people will wound us or our children and there is never an apology or a change. We can wait forever while our wounds fester. But living with bitterness steals our joy—not theirs. And while we do not condone the behavior or words, we do have the opportunity to offer one-sided forgiveness and trust that God will handle the consequences.

That's what we and Morgen ended up doing. It was so hard at first, but we prayed together and forgave the bully. Over time, we watched Morgen have compassion because "hurting people hurt people." She also took ownership of her own tendencies to withdraw and feel sorry for herself that only made things worse. She began to grow.

It was hard for me to forgive. But I knew that was what God was asking. And as we did, we saw why: He doesn't want our hearts to be continually crushed by this type of ongoing difficulty. Sisters, even when it is our children who are being hurt, even when it is one-sided, and even if we have to do it over and over, let's accept this gift of choosing forgiveness from our sweet God.

Reflect

Have you experienced a time when you were more upset about (and had more difficulty forgiving) when a loved one was treated unfairly than when you were being mistreated? Now ponder: our God watched His Son be horribly mistreated, and yet Jesus asked His Father to forgive those people. Which, by extension, includes us who sin against Him every day, despite His sacrifice. And God does forgive us. How can you remember those examples when you see someone you love mistreated? How can you help your loved one do the same?

"Forgiveness means surrendering your right to hurt someone back."

— CHRISTINE CAINE —

Everyone must submit to governing authorities. For all authority comes from God, and those in positions of authority have been placed there by God.

— ROMANS 13:1, NLT

Growing Up

It started when we were toddlers—when we noisily squawked our displeasure at bedtime or mealtime. And we've been declaring our opinions and independence ever since. We think getting what we want will make us happy. So we obey only those boundaries that make sense to us. On the others, we take a page from Pirates of the Caribbean, seeing them more as "guidelines" than actual rules.

We don't realize that what is stirring in the undergrowth is the exact same sin that arose in the Garden: the prideful desire to go our own way. Getting what I want will make me happy. Why should I have to do what someone else says?

Right out of college and newly following Christ, I began attending a great church. With a lifelong passion for musical theater, I was thrilled when the large singles ministry began putting on musicals. We first did Godspell. Next we chose Pippin, which so clearly shows the futility of chasing worldly pleasures to find joy. Pippin ran after drinking, partying, money, wealth, pride, sex—and found only emptiness. It's a powerful lesson.

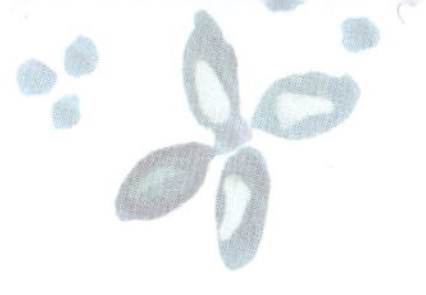

A few months in, after watching us rehearse a few dance numbers, our pastors pulled us aside and gave us a few specific limitations for what could be directly portrayed on the church stage. But we, as brilliant young artists (ahem), got our backs up and protested. It felt so important for the audience to feel the full impact of depravity throughout. We argued, but they insisted. And we showed them: we cancelled the show.

In our pride, we couldn't see the merit of the restrictions—or that we needed the authority of the church. We felt that we were right, and they just didn't understand.

Why should I have to do what someone else says?

How ironic. For the sake of showing the corruption of limitless freedom, we were bucking limits. Our certainty and pride blinded us to the importance of godly authority. I look back at my twenty-three-year-old self and hang my head.

You may have never taken your toys and gone home, just to make a point. But we have all acted like spiritual toddlers. Submitting to authority is a crucial way that God has provided to grow and mature us and give us true joy. Boundaries do far more than keep us from our own destructive folly . . . they also temper our pride. They force us to confront our destructive desire to do things our way.

Father, forgive our rebellion and foolishness and show us how to have hearts of submission, knowing that authority figures in our lives are gifts from Your heart to ours.

Reflect

Pause and think about any authorities that you may have trouble yielding to. (The IRS? Your homeowners association? Your inexperienced boss? The speed limit?) How can choosing faith and reverence for God help you better yield to authority? Ask God for wisdom on what He might want you to change.

"The kind of trust that we are called to give to our fellow imperfect humans in this life, be they family or friends, employers or government officials, or even leaders in a church, can never finally be earned. It must be given as a gift—a gift in faith, in trust more of the God who gives than of the leaders He has given."

— MARK DEVER —

Day 49

Taste and see that the Lord is good.
Oh, the joys of those who take refuge in him!

— PSALM 34:8, NLT

The Year of "Why Not?"

For a year, our family had prayed for the father of one of our closest friends, who was battling cancer. Don had been a highly respected senior executive, and even in retirement, he was a strong Christian witness in a competitive industry. His first wife (my friend's mom) had died years before, and he and his second wife, Patty, had become our friends. They lived in a different state, so we didn't see them often. But we prayed during the long journey of surgeries and chemotherapy and were thrilled when he was pronounced cancer-free.

Not long ago, I asked my friend how her dad and stepmom were doing. She grinned. "They are doing great. They are in Nevis right now."

"Where?"

"Nevis. It's this tiny, remote Caribbean island."

"Really? Why'd they go there?"

My friend started chuckling. "That's what I asked them. And Patty said, 'Why not go there? We've always wanted to go. So we thought:

Why not? This is our year of 'Why not?'" Earlier, they had invited everyone at church who didn't have local family for a Thanksgiving potluck dinner because, well, why not?!

I was so struck by that. During his cancer scare, Don and Patty realized, *We may not have a lot of time left*. They were given the gift of seeing life from a different perspective. So once they realized they *did* have more time, they decided they were going to *purposefully* enjoy the journey. They were going to stop rationalizing away good gifts from the Lord and instead be grateful for those opportunities. They began seriously considering things they would enjoy as a couple. Instead of constantly asking "why" or "can we really do this?" they decided it was time to start declaring, "Why not?"

Sisters, we may not be retired, and we may not have the time or means to go to another country . . . but it doesn't matter! How often have we stopped ourselves from doing something that we would love because it seemed frivolous? Maybe you've always wanted to go to that unfamiliar Vietnamese restaurant and discover what Pho is. Or wished you had the courage to ask a friend to teach you to water ski. Why not try it?

Why not cross the room and introduce yourself to someone new at the office mixer, PTA meeting, or church conference? Why not try for that dream job, watch YouTube videos to learn guitar, or train for a 5K?

How much more joyful would we be if we lived that way most of the time? Let's not wait for the cancer diagnosis or retirement or when the kids have left the house. Let's look to our God, the giver of good gifts, and truly *notice* those "Why not?" gifts He is putting in our path!

Reflect

Imagine that you knew you had limited time left—perhaps a year or two. Jot down some of your dreams in the space below: perhaps a creative project, or cultivating a closer-knit family, or investing in a new friendship. Then ask yourself, "why not now?" and pick several things you want to do in the coming days and months.

"Old ways won't open new doors."

— AUTHOR UNKNOWN —

Day 50

Trust in the LORD with all your heart, and lean not on your own understanding. In all your ways acknowledge Him, and He shall direct your paths.

— PROVERBS 3:5-6, NKJV

My Understanding Has Hurt Feelings

Hailey was twenty-eight years old, had a plan, and was following it. She had prayed about her career and finally knew: she was supposed to become a commercial pilot. She had considered flying fighter jets, but she also wanted to be married someday, and the fighter-pilot life allowed no time to nurture friendships with Christian men.

Hailey was a bit stressed and worried, but she couldn't let that stop her. She enrolled in pilot school 300 miles away from home. With little money, she decided she needed to graduate in the shortest possible time frame and began working two jobs. She was often tired and frustrated but glad to have personal support: she had begun a long-distance relationship with a great guy from home.

Soon, Hailey realized she had drastically underestimated how long it would take to get the necessary flight time—especially during the rainy season. Finally, a week of clear weather was forecasted! She booked three flights and sighed in relief.

The next day she broke her right foot in a freak bicycle accident. Grounded for weeks, she would no longer be able to graduate quickly. Trying not to panic, she called her boyfriend. But something seemed off. Hailey soon discovered what it was: her boyfriend was cheating on her.

Suddenly, everything in her plan for her life—in what she had thought was *God's* plan for her life—was in pieces. In tears, she told God she didn't understand. She was just trying to live out His plan! Surely He saw how hard she had worked to live a holy life in pursuit of Him. Was this what she got in return?

"God," she lamented, "You tell me not to lean on my own understanding, but right now my understanding has hurt feelings!"

Over the next several days, in pain and unable to leave her apartment, Hailey continued to talk to God. And listen. And after a while, the Lord spoke to her heart about her insistence on having to know and control her path. He had come that she might have *life,* and have it more abundantly. But her lack of trust and her desire to micromanage was preventing her from receiving His hope and joy each day—much less any potential changes in His plan. God not only needed to remove "Mr. Wrong" from her life; He also needed to teach her how to trust *His* understanding.

Can you relate? Has your understanding ever had hurt feelings? If we're going to find joy, we have to train ourselves to lean on His understanding, *not* our own. Which means trusting in God with all our heart when we are heartbroken, confused, or can't see the path ahead. After all: that is *faith*!

Reflect

In Proverbs 3:5-6, God tells us how we allow Him to direct our path: we trust Him, we don't rely on our own understanding, and we acknowledge Him in all our ways. Which of those do you struggle with most? If it is trust, search and write down three Scriptures promising that we can trust God. If it's self-reliance, humbly turn over whatever you are planning right now to Him and ask what He wants you to do. If it is that you forget to acknowledge Him, think of one or two strategies you can use to remember to bring Him into every situation.

"God's sovereignty has not been shipwrecked by your storm."

— PRISCILLA SHIRER —

Day 51

Praise the Lord, my soul; all my inmost being, praise his holy name. Praise the Lord, my soul, and forget not all his benefits —who forgives all your sins and heals all your diseases . . . who satisfies your desires with good things.

— PSALM 103:1-3, 5

Forget Not All His Benefits

As a social researcher in the marriage space, I interview a lot of people about their relationships. Clearly, few things bring greater joy into our lives than a great marriage—and few things cause more heartache than a marriage (or any close relationship, really) in a difficult season.

Over the years, dozens of researchers (including us!) have identified one of the greatest success factors for pulling your relationship out of a difficult time, whether that difficult time is multiple years or just an angry day. And I love that it's a principle the Bible has advocated all along—one you're familiar with by now: To stop ourselves from "forgetting" the good and instead purposefully remember the good as a way to restore hope for the future.

In Psalm 103, the psalmist gives us a beautiful example of this, as he works on his relationship with the Lord. The psalms were ordered purposefully, and in the wake of great distress (described in Psalm 102), when he was feeling abandoned by God, the psalmist essentially tells himself: *Praise the Lord. Come on, you can do it—praise Him.* To accomplish this, he begins to list all the amazing things the Lord has done. He reminds himself how God forgives sins, heals diseases, and has given so many good things—which he later lists as well.

He ends *knowing* that the Lord is indeed with him.

When a married couple is struggling, a counselor will often take them back to what attracted them to each other in the first place. They'll talk about the early, happy times in their marriage: good things they did and experienced together. It brings to mind the reasons and the feelings that caused them to fall in love in the first place. It brings back the original joy of their relationship.

Similarly, in our study for *The Surprising Secrets of Highly Happy Marriages,* I was so struck by one of the factors that makes the happiest couples so happy. We've often been told, "Don't keep score," and yet the happiest couples *do* keep score: they keep score of what their spouse is *giving.* Even if it sometimes requires a purposeful effort, they refuse to dwell on the difficulties (which exist for the happy couples just like everyone else!) and instead continuously look for what their spouse is doing that is worthy of praise. And it changes their hearts drastically.[15]

It can change ours as well! So if you're married and having a hard time in your relationship, recall and talk about the times when you and your husband were in harmony. Keep score of the great things your man does. Create your own highlights reel and run it through the projector of your mind to restore your joy.

Reflect

If you are married or in a serious relationship, what are some of your favorite memories of happy times with your significant other? Can you remember a time when strength showed up in your marriage? Romance? Fun and laughter? Record some of these memories below, and pray for God to help restore your joy. If you are not married, is there a friend with whom you have a strained relationship? How can remembering your times of good friendship help you overcome the strain? Ask God to give you a heart of love for your friend and send them a card or give them a call.

"May you never forget what is worth remembering, nor ever remember what is best forgotten."

— IRISH BLESSING —

Day 52

But if you do not forgive others their sins,
your Father will not forgive your sins.

— MATTHEW 6:15

Forgive Them; Forgive Us

Years ago, our friends Isabelle and Zack were finally able to breathe financially. God had always provided, but it had always been tight. Then their closest friend at church, Sebastian, a very successful fund manager, offered to help them and other church members by allowing them into a prosperous investment pool. The returns were great, and Isabelle was ecstatic. She and Zack invested most of their savings and brought in twenty-five other church members, who together invested millions. Church was now not just a spiritual blessing; it was a business network that would help people prosper. Or so it seemed. One day, FBI agents came knocking. Isabelle and Zack assured them that Sebastian couldn't be involved in fraud and cover-ups. He was a godly church leader. Their monthly statements showed solid profits.

A few months later, in a courtroom filled with shocked and betrayed church members, Sebastian was found guilty of running a Ponzi scheme and sentenced to decades in prison.

Isabelle and Zack's anger was particularly complicated; they had no idea how to forgive and get back to a life of contentment. Sebastian had victimized not only them, but a great many whom they recruited.

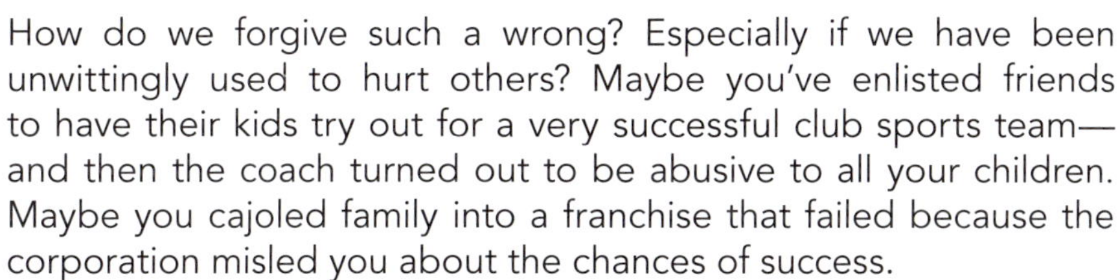

How do we forgive such a wrong? Especially if we have been unwittingly used to hurt others? Maybe you've enlisted friends to have their kids try out for a very successful club sports team—and then the coach turned out to be abusive to all your children. Maybe you cajoled family into a franchise that failed because the corporation misled you about the chances of success.

It's complicated anger. Which, sometimes, may be a signal that we not only need to forgive the wrong-doer, but have a need for forgiveness ourselves.

Isabelle and Zack felt God showing them some hard truths: They weren't pure victims. Their hearts had grown cold—and greedy. They loved the high returns and were glad for others to see them "living the life." They enjoyed the accolades that came from introducing others to worldly success. Worse still, they had violated God's heart for a church. In Matthew 21:13 (NLT) Jesus said, "The Scriptures declare, 'My Temple will be called a house of prayer,' but you have turned it into a den of thieves!"

The pain of this realization was almost unbearable, but God brought them through repentance and back to peace.

Sisters, sometimes we must forgive pure wrongdoing against us. But sometimes we must recognize our own part in the drama and our own need for forgiveness. Let us never shy away from hard truths. God will never waste our pain or mistakes. He redeems them as we learn to forgive—and be forgiven.

Reflect

A Matthew 18 parable illustrates how negatively God feels about a person who, after being forgiven a huge and unpayable debt, will not forgive his fellow man a comparably small amount. Are you finding it hard to forgive someone today? Because each of us is flawed, rarely does the blame in a conflict reside 100 percent with one person. Even if your share is only 10 percent, consider how you could have responded differently, then ask God for His forgiveness and for a willing heart to forgive the other person.

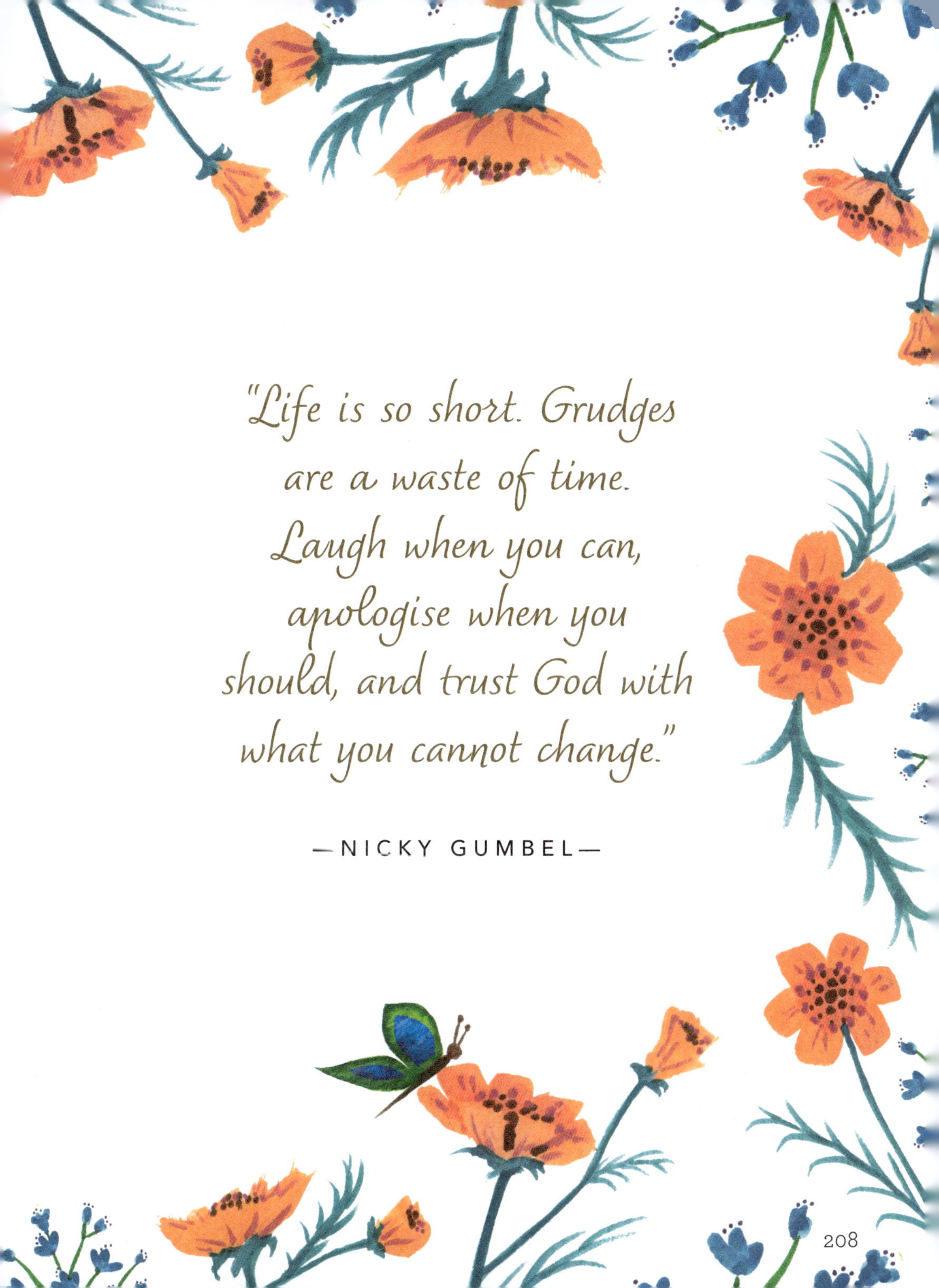

"Life is so short. Grudges are a waste of time. Laugh when you can, apologise when you should, and trust God with what you cannot change."

—NICKY GUMBEL—

Day 53

But may all who search for you be filled with joy and gladness in you. May those who love your salvation repeatedly shout, "The LORD is great!"

— PSALM 40:16, NLT

Joy in the Journey

One hundred and sixty-nine miles. That is the distance Ellie drove her kids in *one day.* Multiple times a week. Just for after-school activities. Many of us have been there, right? Whether we are commuting, driving toddlers to preschool or older students to volleyball or youth group—or all of the above—many women can relate to spending lots of time in the car.

It is easy to start feeling, *I was made for more than this.* To feel burdened. Put upon.

Ellie had originally started tracking her miles for fun. But watching the odometer tick over soon brought frustration. Every time she got into the driver's seat, dread bubbled to the surface. And if her children acted irritable about being in the car for so long, watch out! Long gone was the compassionate mom—she was replaced by an on-edge woman who snapped that it was their choice to do the activities, not hers.

One particular day, the traffic was horrible, her girls were grumpy, and they were late. Ellie was fed up. She dropped them off and decided to walk outside instead of trying to cram in an errand. She walked along, discouraged and stressed . . . and then it started to rain.

She finally looked up to the sky to talk to God about this. (Because, really? Rain? Now?!) That's when she noticed that *it was raining only on her.* What a perfect message from God about her mood. But more importantly, she was stunned to see that the rest of the sky was filled with indescribable, movie-worthy clouds. If it had not started raining, she would not have paused to look up and see this glorious sight.

Thank you, God, she whispered. *Thank you for forcing me to pause and see this.*

She took tons of pictures, eager to share them with her girls. Then she realized: the beauty had not only caused her to pause her discouragement long enough to see something worthy of praise, it had also caused her to turn her thoughts to something she could show her kids, something they could praise God for as well.

She also realized something else. Those cloud formations had probably been there during her whole drive, and she had totally missed them. What would happen if she stopped dreading each drive and started eagerly looking for what God would show her that day?

Sisters, how often is there such beauty above us—something we miss until God sends a little rainstorm to wake us up? The next time we are on our last nerve because of an unexpected delay, a broken-down car, or an interruption in a packed schedule, look up. Let's *look* for what God is trying to show us that will give us joy in the journey.

Reflect

Is there a chore, commute, after-school schedule, or some other commitment that currently feels like a burden? What might make the obligation less draining and more joyful? What might God want to show you if you look for it? Write some thoughts below.

"Blessed are they who see beautiful things in humble places where other people see nothing."

—CAMILLE PISSARRO—

Day 54

After the earthquake came a fire, but the Lord was not in the fire. And after the fire came a gentle whisper.

—1 KINGS 19:12

Earthquakes, Fires, and Gentle Whispers

In 2010, a devastating earthquake struck Haiti, killing or leaving homeless hundreds of thousands of people. Thousands of Christian young people—including our goddaughter, Sarah—set aside college classes or jobs and helped with the recovery effort. At the time, Sarah was studying at an urban college, dating a young man, and pondering her future.

The devastation in Haiti put a lot of her questions into perspective. Suddenly, she was surrounded by deep grief and needs that cried to be met with few resources: *We only have so much time and money! In this hour, do we organize this housing for American mission teams, or do we help at these particular ministry sites?* There was a lot of seeking the Lord in an entirely new way: *Lord, what should we do NOW?*

The team was beleaguered by unbearable heat, infections, the smell of burning garbage, and the chanting of witch doctors. They even ran out of food. *What should we do NOW?* For a few days the team ate the protein bars Sarah's mother had stuffed inside her guitar case.

Yet in the midst of it all, Sarah and her team felt the amazing peace that comes from *having* to rely on and hear the gentle whispers from God.

With all the distractions from her regular life stripped away, Sarah decided to pray about the things that had been puzzling her in the US. But when she heard that gentle whisper, it wasn't what she expected. *It is time for you to break up with your boyfriend. He's not the one I've chosen for you.*

Shocked, Sarah recorded that in her journal, started praying about it . . . and felt that same sense of peace that this was God's direction for what to do NOW. So once back home, she obeyed God and made some big changes. And very soon, she met Philip, the amazing man who would eventually become her husband. She was so grateful that God had taught her how to hear His gentle whisper during such a challenging time.

During the COVID-19 pandemic that swept the world in 2020, many of us saw for ourselves the difference it makes when we are not in the clutter and comfort of our regular lives. During "normal" times, it is easy to get distracted and miss that still, small whisper. And yet God is still there, still speaking. We don't need to experience an earthquake to hear Him, but let us act as if we have. Let us recognize our deep need for His direction, every day, on what we should do NOW, and trust that when it is needed, we will hear Him.

Reflect

"The Lord confides in those who fear him" (Psalm 25:14). God desires to lead us as much as we desire to be led. The question is, how much do we desire it? Enough to remove things that distract us, to earnestly pray for His guidance—and then prioritize obedience over our own plans? If you're longing to hear from God today, ask Him to help you honor Him more. Take a moment to read Psalm 25 as a personal prayer to God.

"Earthly wisdom is doing what comes naturally. Godly wisdom is doing what the Holy Spirit compels us to do."

— CHARLES STANLEY —

Day 55

And we know that God causes everything to work together for the good of those who love God and are called according to his purpose for them.

— ROMANS 8:28, NLT

Unspeakable Pain—Unspeakable Joy

I was in tears as I read a blog by a mom who had lost her young son in a tragic car accident. I soon saw another by a dad who lost his daughter to cancer at age four. More tears. Goodness, I had to read something else! Later that day, an email came about a neighbor who died unexpectedly, leaving his wife to raise two children alone.

Oh, the heartache of these people. But in their responses, I began to see something else. A pattern. All three were facing raw pain with amazing grace. In different ways, each stated a trust in God's love and gratitude for all that He had done. They thanked Him for the time they had with their loved one. For awareness of the need to live each day fully. For His indescribable peace when everything shattered. Yes, they expressed anger and asked why. But those moments were always followed with, *"But I trust You, Lord. Your will, not mine. I don't like this, but please use it for Your glory."*

They seemed to have joy . . . even in unspeakable pain. But how?

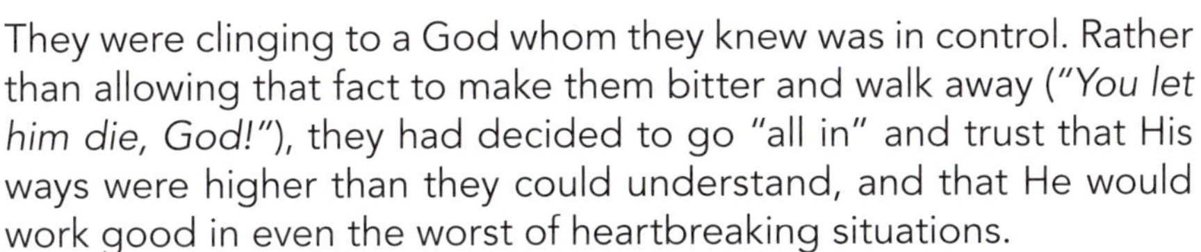

They were clinging to a God whom they knew was in control. Rather than allowing that fact to make them bitter and walk away (*"You let him die, God!"*), they had decided to go "all in" and trust that His ways were higher than they could understand, and that He would work good in even the worst of heartbreaking situations.

You and I may not have faced those specific tragedies. But we've all been overwhelmed. We've all wondered why God would allow a horrible thing to happen. We may not have known how we would get through a time of darkness.

Romans 8:28 helps so much when we confront things we do not understand. But for these amazing parents, it clearly is not just about "getting through" something. Our God speaks hope in times that seem hopeless. He provides a promise when our world has completely changed—a promise that He overcomes the darkness.

And that message is explosive. It is why the gospel, as seen in the lives of persecuted, loving, joyful people, spread throughout the world. As I read through the responses to the blogs of those who lost their children, I saw that so strongly. People said things like, "You are showing me what the love of God really means in a way that I have never seen before," and, "That you can have peace today must mean that Jesus is real."

We cannot fathom God's ways. But sometimes we glimpse how He uses even the unfathomably hard times. As one of those parents said: knowing that others were finding Christ—that was a joy that could never be explained. In the midst of unspeakable pain, unspeakable joy.

Reflect

Are you in need of help to find joy amidst your or a loved one's pain? Did you know that God has given us a pattern for handling pain in the book of Psalms, roughly one-third of which are songs of lament? Read Psalm 13 (it's only 6 verses) and note the psalmist's progression, from pouring out deep emotion, to asking God for help, to declaring trust in God, ending in affirmation of God's goodness. Using this pattern, write a psalm of your own today.

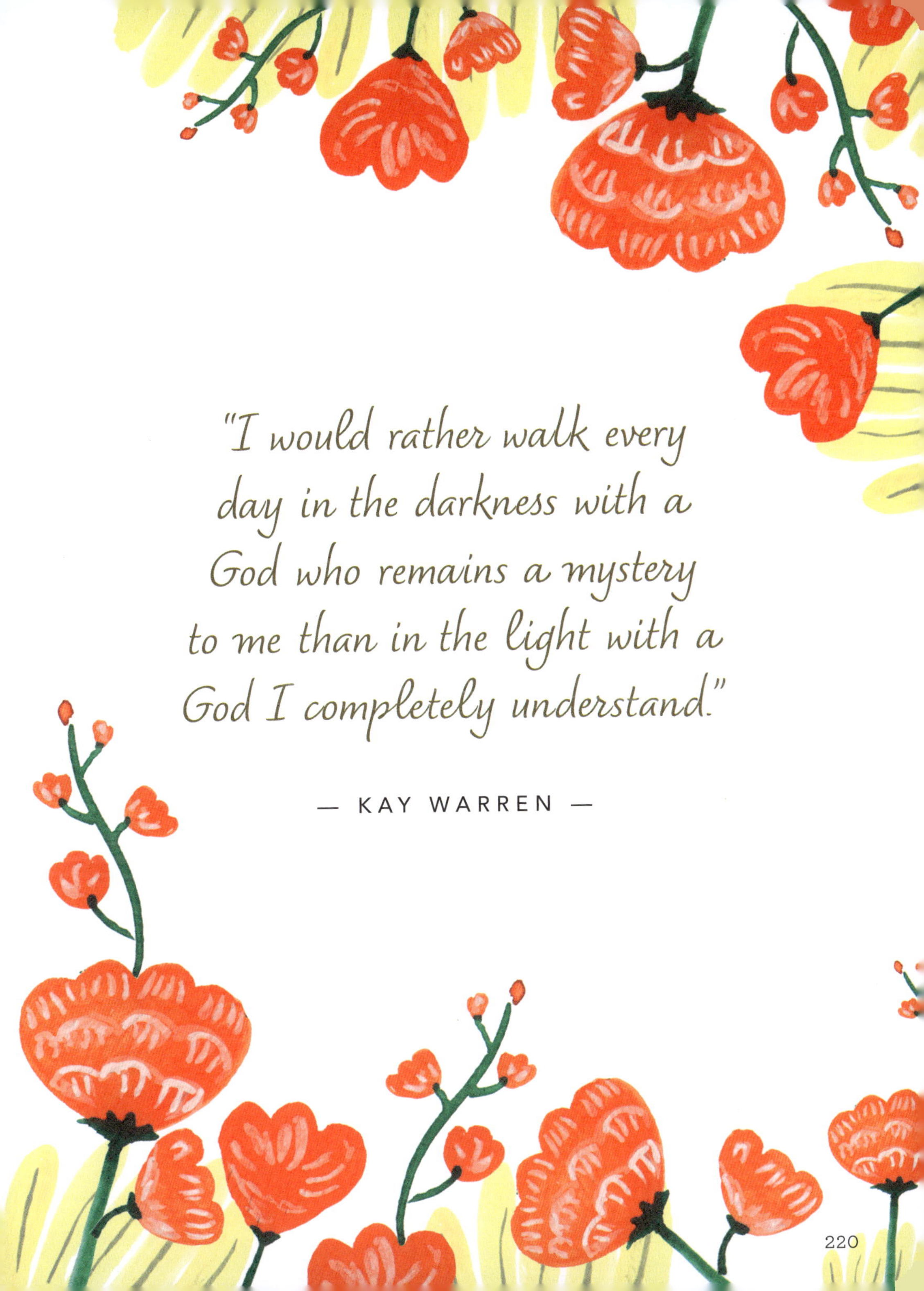

"I would rather walk every day in the darkness with a God who remains a mystery to me than in the light with a God I completely understand."

— KAY WARREN —

Day 56

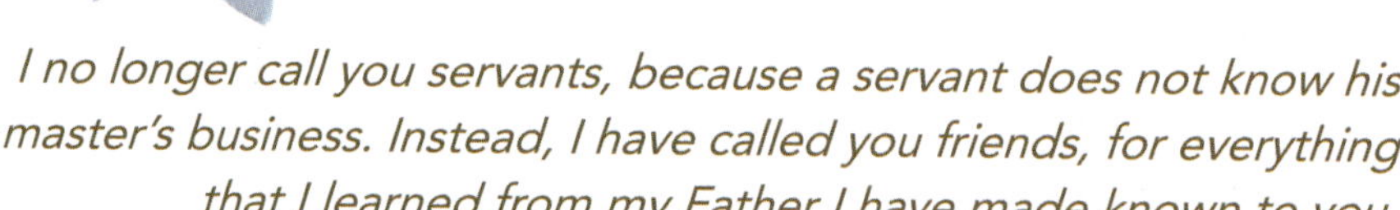

I no longer call you servants, because a servant does not know his master's business. Instead, I have called you friends, for everything that I learned from my Father I have made known to you.

— JOHN 15:15

Hearing Him as a Friend

I love the movie *The King's Speech*, the true story of King George VI, who began ruling Great Britain at the outset of World War II. Hidden in the plot is a beautiful example of the relationship our God wants with us.

A bit of background: When King George's father died, the oldest son, Edward, originally ascended the throne. But he was more interested in dallying with a married American woman than he was in confronting Adolf Hitler. Soon, he abdicated the throne to his brother Albert (also known as "Bertie"), who became King George VI.

In the modern era, the main role of the royal family was speaking to and for the people. Rallying and reassuring everyone had never been more important, to confront the Nazi menace and get through the hard war years to come. But Bertie had a severe, almost incapacitating stammer whenever he tried to speak publicly. Many doctors and speech therapists had been unable to help. How could the king rally his people when he was unable to do a public broadcast?

The answer came from a man who started as a speech therapist and became a dear friend to the king.

Lionel Logue did things differently. He wouldn't come to the palace. He wouldn't be a servant or a doctor-for-hire. Instead, the king would need to go to Logue's office, and eventually his home, where Logue would not just teach the mechanics of speaking, but be a listening ear to the sovereign. Logue knew that stammers are caused by deep, undealt-with fears. The king had to know Lionel was there for him so he could open up and unburden himself of his fears.

They had to move from being "Your Majesty" and "Dr. Logue" to being simply Bertie and Lionel. Two friends.

They did. And with Lionel's support and help, Bertie overcame his stammer. His many wartime speeches kept the English courage and spirit alive. And Lionel was at his right hand for all of them. The king wanted his friend close.

It is amazing to think that we aren't just servants to our King. Our God invites us—US!—to be there *as His friends.* Now, unlike Bertie or any earthly king, God doesn't need our help. But He does want us to enjoy Him in a new way. Jesus said, "I no longer call you servants. . . . I have called you friends."

Yes, our God is deserving of our service and devotion. But He has invited us into a deep and abiding friendship with Him as well. He wants us to hear from Him and share with Him as friends. Let us accept the invitation!

Reflect

If you want to build a friendship with someone, list four or five things that you need to do. Looking at the list, are those same things important to building your friendship with God? In the months to come, how can you do each of those things?

"Every friendship with God and every love between Him and a soul is the only one of its kind."

— JANET ERSKINE STUART —

Day 57

God will do this, for he is faithful to do what he says, and he has invited you into partnership with his Son, Jesus Christ our Lord.

— 1 CORINTHIANS 1:9, NLT

His Real Promises

I met my friend Catherine on the first day of school when our boys started fifth grade. She was new, and we struck up a conversation. I was intrigued when she said she had three kids but any day would hopefully have five.

Catherine and her husband soon welcomed two young children from foster care. And I watched an amazing, anxious, beautiful journey unfold.

Catherine knew foster care is ultimately meant to reunite children with their biological parents. She knew it in her head and believed in it if it was best for the kids, but her heart . . . oh, her heart was torn. She was rooting for the biological parents. But these sweet children—she was rooting for their well-being, too.

Their church wrapped around Catherine's family. Meals, support, babysitting, rides to therapy. They saw the children thriving, got to know them in Sunday school, the nursery, and kid's choir. They couldn't help but ask about their future. Catherine repeatedly said, "The situation is in God's hands, but the court is likely to send the kids home."

That's when well-meaning friends would lovingly pat Catherine's arm and tell her, "God has promised you these kids. Your family is what's best for them." Catherine appreciated the support, but her heart broke each time. She kept thinking, *How can anyone say that? God did not promise me these kids. There is nowhere in the Bible that promises that I'll always get the outcome I want.*

When we are in a season of waiting or worry, it is so easy for our anxious hearts to cling to a particular hope as if it is a promise from God. Which means we risk being devastated if God does not deliver what we want. Yet at the exact same time, our God has made many explosive, life-transforming promises that are *real*. We must cling to those!

Catherine took that path. She told herself, *God did not promise me any one outcome. But He did promise me that He will never leave me or forsake me—or these children* (Deuteronomy 31:6). *He will strengthen me* (Isaiah 41:10). *He will work things together for my good because I love Him* (Romans 8:28). *When I pass through the waters, He will be with me* (Isaiah 43:2). *He will be with me—and them—wherever we go* (Joshua 1:9).

Catherine clung to those *real* promises. And I watched her live for the next two years with the tension of not knowing, yet still broadcasting an inexplicable joy—a joy that rises up once we recognize that God has great power and a great plan that overshadows any heartache this world can throw at us.

God is a God of big promises. Real ones.

Reflect

When we place our hope in particular outcomes, we presume to know more than God about what the future holds and what is best. But when we base our peace on the promises of God for us, we have built our faith upon bedrock. Which of the biblical promises Catherine clung to do you also need to trust today? Look up one of the verses and rewrite it in your own words, personalizing it to your situation. Then pray, asking God to help you believe that He and His grace will be there for you—no matter what your future holds.

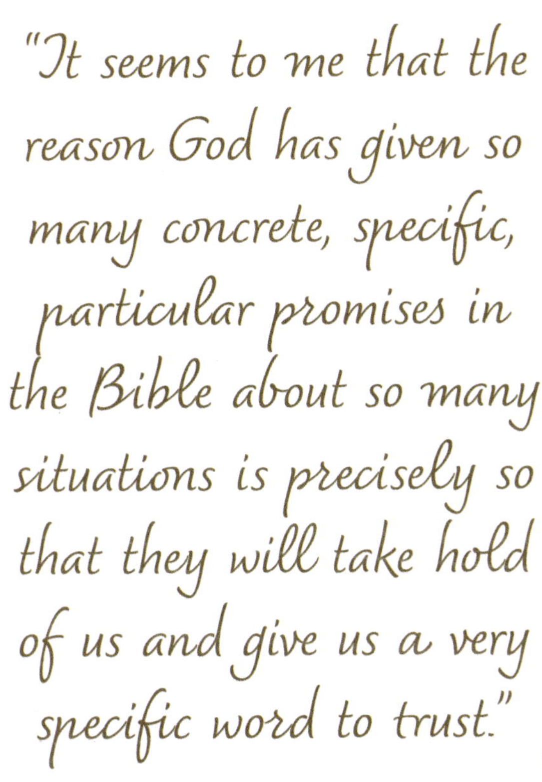
"It seems to me that the
reason God has given so
many concrete, specific,
particular promises in
the Bible about so many
situations is precisely so
that they will take hold
of us and give us a very
specific word to trust."

— JOHN PIPER —

Day 58

Count it all joy . . . when you meet trials of various kinds, for you know that the testing of your faith produces steadfastness. And let steadfastness have its full effect, that you may be perfect and complete, lacking in nothing.

— JAMES 1:2-4, ESV

In All Circumstances

The book *The Hiding Place* is the autobiography of Corrie ten Boom, who survived a concentration camp in World War II. Corrie and her family were devout Christians arrested for hiding Jews during the Nazi invasion of the Netherlands.

In the camp, Corrie and her older sister, Betsie, huddled together in the deplorable, overcrowded barracks, stomachs aching from lack of food, sleeping on rotting straw ridden with fleas. But Betsie encouraged Corrie to give thanks for everything: "Thank you, Lord, for being kept together in the concentration camp. Thank you, Lord, for our Bible not being taken from us. Thank you, Lord, for so many women in such a small space, because it is all the more who will get to hear the Word of God from us! Thank you, Lord, for the fleas."

Wait, what? Corrie was skeptical about giving thanks for fleas. (Could you? I mean, *fleas?!*) But Betsie did—since God says to "give thanks in *ALL* circumstances."

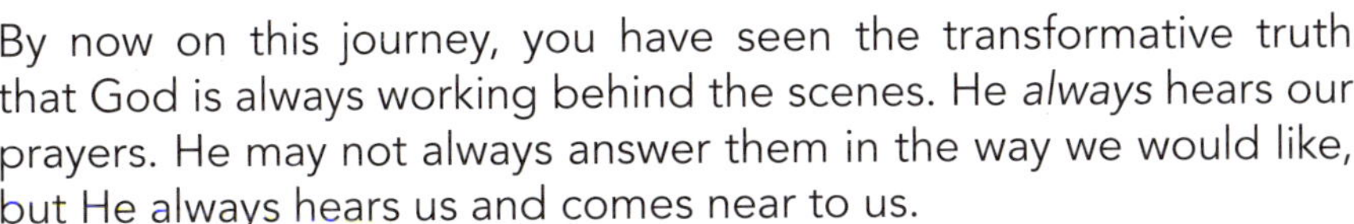

By now on this journey, you have seen the transformative truth that God is always working behind the scenes. He *always* hears our prayers. He may not always answer them in the way we would like, but He always hears us and comes near to us.

He also can bring joy even in the most miserable of places, especially when we give thanks in faith while not being able to *imagine* how God could use something for His purposes—and watch for what God might be doing in the midst of it all.

In their overcrowded barracks, Corrie and Betsie began holding worship services and Bible studies. They were surprised the guards never came to stop them, but they later learned it was because none of the guards wanted to risk the vermin! There truly *had* been reason to give thanks for the fleas.[16]

One of the "next steps" for us in our growth in joy is what we *default* to when we are faced with hard circumstances beyond our control or comprehension. When we face a serious health concern, potential eviction, failed work project, or struggling relationship, have we practiced gratitude enough that we default to giving thanks instead of sadness, anger, or complaining? If we're not quite there yet, let us keep practicing the habit of thanking God for *all* of it until that becomes our default.

We may not always get the answers we want. But each time, every time, there *will* be joy waiting for us as we trust in a God who knows the bigger picture.

Reflect

Try to remember and list the last few occasions when you experienced hardship, irritation, or an area of worry. In which cases did you practice giving thanks, trusting that God was there, and that His hand was working behind the scenes? Thank God for helping you to do that, and ask Him to help you do that more and more in the months to come.

"What separates privilege from entitlement is gratitude."

— BRENÉ BROWN —

Day 59

Unless the Lord *builds a house, the work of the builders is wasted. Unless the* Lord *protects a city, guarding it with sentries will do no good. It is useless for you to work so hard from early morning until late at night, anxiously working for food to eat; for God gives rest to his loved ones. Children are a gift from the* Lord *. . . [they] are like arrows in a warrior's hands. How joyful is the man whose quiver is full of them!*

— PSALM 127:1-5, NLT

Too Busy for Gifts?

Sisters, we *know* that children—whether biological, adopted, or spiritual children—are gifts from the Lord. But are we too busy to truly be "joyful" in them? To truly enjoy them as gifts?

Am I working from morning until night? Check. Sometimes anxious and stressed? Check. Needing and longing for rest? Check. Check. Already, as I read these words, I find myself wanting to lean into God's promise of rest, even as I don't know how I would get everything done.

But then I talk myself out of it. Because it's just a little stress, right? Just a lack of sleep. Thanks, God, but there's so much to do and it is for my family! And why does our craziness matter, anyway?

This is where the lesson begins. Why does it matter? Because "Children are a gift from the Lord . . . how joyful is the man whose quiver is full of them!"

If we imagine our family as a city, there are so many things required to keep it functioning. Jobs, meal-planning, homework, after-school activities, youth group, sports, chores—and let's not forget sleeping. Our little city resembles Times Square! And in the bustle, all the good family and household things can feel like a burden rather than a joy. "I have to do this or it will all fall apart."

Unless the Lord protects a city, guarding it with sentries will do no good.

Sisters, we've learned so much these last weeks. Have we come to grips with one of the most important lessons to *ongoing* joy? It is *God's* job to protect and run our family, not ours! We must be able to trust Him with our schedules, our needs, our worries, and those we love. It is *His job* to make sure it will not all fall apart—not ours.

Sure, He wants us to steward our gifts well. But that's the key: our family, our time, our schedules, even our to-do lists: *they are gifts from God to us.* They are meant to be *enjoyed.*

As we ponder the weeks and months ahead, let us take the lessons we have learned already and use them to relax, take a deep breath, and tell God thanks for all that He's given us—for joy.

Reflect

What gifts has God given you that you might be too busy or anxious to enjoy? And what lie are you believing that is keeping you from enjoying them? (For example, "If I don't do it, it will all fall apart.") List the most important gifts and call out the lie(s). Thank God for those gifts and ask Him to show you: How can you be a good steward of what God has given you while also trusting Him to "protect your city" so you can enjoy those gifts as well?

"You will never look back on life and think, 'I've spent too much time with my kids.'"

— AUTHOR UNKNOWN —

Day 60

You make known to me the path of life; in your presence there is fullness of joy; at your right hand are pleasures forevermore.

— PSALM 16:11, ESV

The Beautiful Road Map

I have a picture in my mind. I am a teenager, walking along a white sand beach in Hawaii, hand in hand with my father. He and my mom scrimped, saved, and used frequent flyer miles to fly themselves, me, and my brother to Hawaii for Christmas.

Nothing could prepare me for what I saw as we traveled around the area where we were staying. I had seen pictures and videos. I had read guidebooks and imagined it in my mind. But until I experienced the deep blue ocean and towering green mountains firsthand, I could not comprehend how profoundly beautiful it was. Just as in the example I shared on day one of this journey, I was filled with awe. Now that I had experienced it, I could finally understand what everyone had been trying to explain.

Here's the thing: Joy is like that, too. The Bible is our road map and guide to a depth of beauty in our relationship with God that is almost inexplicable. Many verses act as signposts to finding that joy. And when you experience that joy even in the face of sorrow or uncertainty, there is simply nothing like it. It is truly a mystery—a gift from God.

It also points us to another mystery, one that right now, we can only imagine in our minds: the glory of heaven.

Sisters, as much as we are called to pursue and find joy here, this world is not our home. Here, our joy will inevitably be shadowed. But in eternity, in the presence of God, there will be no shadows. There will be none of the pain and loss that stalks our world (Revelation 21:4). Think of it: we will join in the worship of Jesus with the same angels who declared the "good news of great joy" two thousand years ago!

That should be our ultimate source of true joy. We will see Him face-to-face.

In *The Last Battle*, C. S. Lewis describes heaven as "more real and more beautiful" than the world we are living in. He paints a picture of crossing over into eternal life and discovering more and more wonder with every step. "Further up, and further in!" is the cry.[17]

We are called to press into our relationship with Him here, even as we long for the day when there is nothing between us.

That is where my sweet dad is now. After a devastating stroke and a two-year battle, he is walking with Jesus. It makes me ache with joy to think of what he is experiencing.

It also makes me ache with joy to think that someday, I'll be able to walk hand in hand with my dad again.

That is the true joy that God has for all of us who follow Jesus. It is something that is impossible to fully explain until we have taken that step of surrender (such as the prayer on page 246). But it is very real. Friends, as we have traveled together during these past sixty days, I pray that this journey to joy has been a blessing to you. And I pray it continues. Keep following the road map. Fill your heart with the wonder of God. Notice, remember, and be grateful for all that He does for you. Spend time with Him, know Him, and trust that His plan is good in all ways. Always.

Experience it for yourself and let the joy within you be a light to others.

Thanks for joining us on the journey.

"My home is Heaven.
I'm just traveling
through this world."

— BILLY GRAHAM —

Questions to Consider for the Days Ahead

What are the most important blessings you have seen during this journey? Thank God for what He has done during this time.

Thinking back on all God has shown you in the last few months, what are the two or three main areas in which you have most grown? How are you finding joy in ways you were not before?

What are some actions, attitudes, or habits you know that you still need to work on or have left undone, that you feel God is asking you to address?

What actions, attitudes, or habits do you think you're starting to do well, that God is asking you to continue?

Of all the items listed, what are the most important two or three *specific* action steps that you feel God would have you do or continue in the days and months ahead? (For example: "I need to read my Bible and pray every day *before* I take a shower, because I know I won't do so afterward once I get busy with the day.") Don't take this lightly. Take some time to think and pray about it. Then, if you feel like you can make a commitment to God, pray, make that commitment now, and write those two or three action steps here. Come back here in the coming weeks and note what happens as you step out in these areas and continue to grow.

"Further up and further in!"

— C.S. LEWIS, THE LAST BATTLE —

Accepting Jesus' Salvation —and Deciding to Follow Him

Have you ever truly accepted the salvation offered in Jesus? If not, or if you're not sure, look up Romans 3:10 and 6:23 and then the words of Jesus to you in John 3:16 and 10:10. Do you want that kind of joy? That LIFE? If so, write a prayer to Jesus telling Him so, and accepting His forgiveness and salvation. (If you need an example, see the prayer on the next page.)

Then, truly *follow* Jesus. Reach out to a Bible-believing church nearby that can help you grow in your faith and joy. Keep reading the Bible regularly, and take steps to grow in Christ. I suggest you download the free iDisciple app for wonderful resources that can help you in your Christian life!

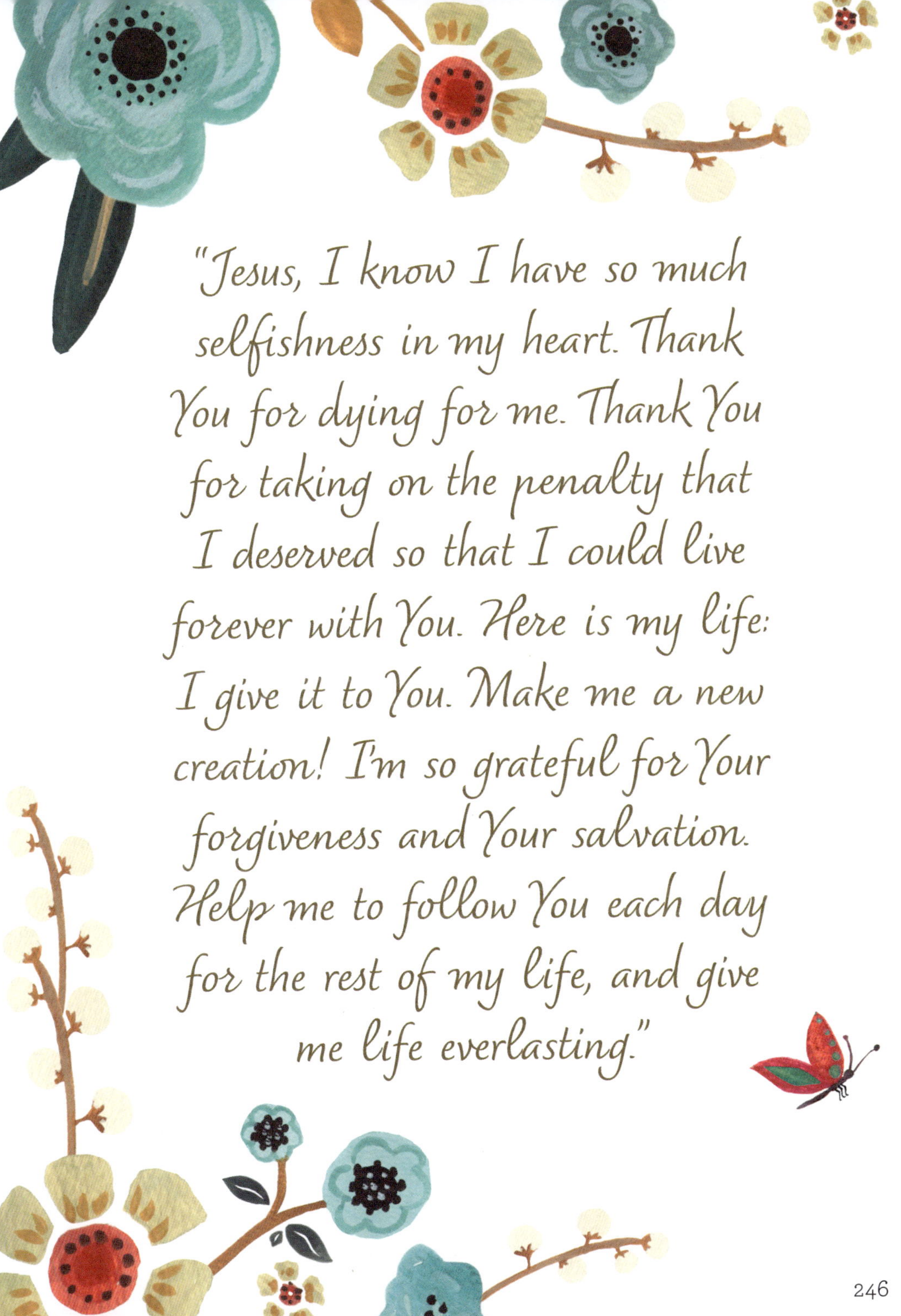

"Jesus, I know I have so much selfishness in my heart. Thank You for dying for me. Thank You for taking on the penalty that I deserved so that I could live forever with You. Here is my life: I give it to You. Make me a new creation! I'm so grateful for Your forgiveness and Your salvation. Help me to follow You each day for the rest of my life, and give me life everlasting."

With my thanks...

Many wonderful people have gone with me on my own personal journey to find joy during a difficult season as I was writing this devotional, especially with the loss of my father. There is simply not enough space to list everyone, but know that you have my heartfelt love and thanks.

As always, I'm so very grateful to the iDisciple/Giving Company team, and thrilled to see how God has expanded your publishing ministry. To David Henriksen, Kobus Johnsen, John Smith, Shawna Brown, and the rest: I am so blessed to work with you—and find joy just by hanging out with you guys! To Nancy Taylor, our brilliant editor: thank you so much for yet again guiding this project from wordiness to clarity. A big shout out to Alli Worthington for your beautiful Foreword.

And speaking of beautiful, to our outstanding artist, Annabelle Grobler, you make these "Find Series" projects come alive. It makes me joyful just to look at what you do!

To my team: You all are rock stars with humble hearts, and I could do none of this without you. Katie Phillips, you are a brilliant writer, editor, coordinator, friend . . . and now a fellow author. I couldn't be more joyful for you! Charlyn Elliott, I'm in awe of not only your writing and management ability, but of your heart for the Lord in the midst of the madness. To the rest of the writing team, including my dear friends Lisa Rice and Julie Fidler, my senior researcher Tally Whitehead, and brilliant writers Beth Peazzoni, Melinda Verdesca, Brooke Turbyfill, and Emily McEntyre: many thanks for using your God-given talents to transform my voice and email notes into meaningful words. Your love for Christ and commitment to finding joy even in the midst of ever-changing deadlines and priorities, illnesses, and obstacles shines through all that you do. A special thanks goes to the rest of my team, Eileen Kirkland and Caroline Niziol, who excel at keeping things running while I am in the middle of writing and speaking projects, as well as to the dozens of men and women on our prayer team who lifted up this whole devotional process. I'm so very grateful for you!

To Jeff, Morgen, and Luke: You fill my world with love, joy, and delight every day. To my mom, Judy Reidinger, who is a living testimony to finding joy even amidst the sadness of watching my earthly dad move to his heavenly home. And in special remembrance of Naomi Duncan—a true sister in Christ, dedicated co-worker, and friend. Our earthly hearts are broken, yet filled with joy over knowing you are with Jesus, your hero and our Savior. This book is dedicated to you.

Finally, I give all the glory to my Heavenly Father who is the true, everlasting source of joy.

— Shaunti Feldhahn

Sources

DAY 1 — C. S. Lewis, *The Problem of Pain* (New York: Harper One, 2015), 47.

DAY 2 — James Clear, Twitter, August 5, 2019, https://twitter.com/JamesClear/status/1158375922845835270.

DAY 3 — https://sermonquotes.com/authors/charles-spurgeon/8497-while-others-are-congratulating-themselves.html.

DAY 4 — Randy Smith, Sermon: "Wholehearted Trust," Proverbs 3:5-6, December 26, 2004; https://gracequotes.org.

DAY 5 — https://www.azquotes.com/quote/424431.

DAY 6 — https://www.bible.com/reading-plans/8721-whisper-how-hear-the-voice-of-god-mark-batterson/day/2.

DAY 7 — Sam Storms, *Pleasures Evermore: The Life-Changing Power of Knowing God* (Colorado Springs, CO: *Navpress*, 2000), 75.

DAY 8 — Lysa Terkeurst, *Am I Messing Up My Kids? . . . and Other Questions Every Mom Asks* (Eugene, OR: Harvest House, 2010), 208.

DAY 9 — https://www.azquotes.com/quote/434046.

DAY 10 — Charles Spurgeon, *Spurgeon's Sermon Notes* (Grand Rapids, MI: Kregel, 1990), 77.

DAY 11 — https://quotefancy.com/quote/1578584/Walter-Anderson-Sadly-some-folks-want-others-to-feel-their-pain-to-hurt-as-much-as-they.

DAY 12 — Rick Warren, "Trusting God When You Don't Understand," personal blog, November 23, 2019, https://pastorrick.com/trusting-god-when-you-dont-understand/.

DAY 13 — Elisabeth Elliott, *The Path of Loneliness: Finding Your Way through the Wilderness to God* (Revel, 2007), https://www.goodreads.com/work/quotes/147519.

DAY 14 — https://quoteinvestigator.com/2019/04/18/staircase/amp/.

DAY 15 — JamilynHull.com.

DAY 16 — Matthew 25:40, NLT.

DAY 17 — Author unknown

DAY 18 — https://wisdomquotes.com/gratitude-quotes/.

DAY 19 — https://quotesblog.net/those-who-leave-everything-in-gods-hand-will-eventually-see/.

DAY 20 — Lysa TerKeurst, *Unglued: Making Wise Choices in the Midst of Raw Emotions* (Thomas Nelson, 2012); https://www.goodreads.com/quotes/7304708-do-not-check-in-with-the-screaming-demands-of-the.

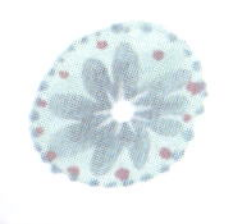

Sources

DAY 21 — Ray Ortlund, "Going Soft Against Wrath," desiringgod.org, May 28, 2013, https://www.desiringgod.org/articles/going-soft-against-wrath.

DAY 22 — Quoted in Dr. Glenn E. Clifton, *The Glorious Grace of God Unveiled* (Bloomington, IN: Westbow Press, 2017), https://gracequotes.org.

DAY 23 — Ann Voskamp, *One Thousand Gifts: A Dare to Live Fully Right Where You Are* (Zondervan, 2010), 139.

DAY 24 — Rick Warren, *The Purpose-Driven Life* (Grand Rapids, Michigan: Zondervan, 2007), 67.

DAY 25 — Philip Yancey, *Prayer: Does It Make Any Difference* (Grand Rapids, MI: Zondervan, 2006), 210.

DAY 26 — https://www.brainyquote.com/quotes/rose_kennedy_134996.

DAY 27 — John H. Putnam, *He Spends, She Spends: Why God Wants You to Live for Free* (Fedd Books, 2016), 73.

DAY 28 — https://i.pinimg.com/originals/91/13/fc/9113fcc890a8460212abc63b56427776.jpg.

DAY 29 — https://www.goodreads.com/quotes/149380-hope-is-believing-in-spite-of-the-evidence-and-then.

DAY 30 — https://www.goodreads.com/work/quotes/147519-the-path-of-loneliness-finding-your-way-through-the-wilderness-to-god.

DAY 31 — Robert Morris, "Call for Confirmation," sermons.love, https://sermons.love/robert-morris-sermons/frequency/3626-robert-morris-call-for-confirmation.html.

DAY 32 — Paraphrase of words by Mother Teresa, https://motherteresa.org/08_info/Quotesf.html.

DAY 33 — https://www.goodreads.com/work/quotes/43254800 through-the-eyes-of-a-lion-facing-impossible-pain-finding-incredible-p.

DAY 34 — John Charles Ryle, *Practical Religion* (Grand Rapids: Baker Book House), 61.

DAY 35 — https://www.elijahnotes.com/powerful-christian-quotes/.

DAY 36 — https://www.goodreads.com/quotes/63433.

DAY 37 — Tim Keller, Twitter, November 6, 2017, https://twitter.com/timkellernyc/status/927619168995823616.

DAY 38 — Mary Elizabeth Williams, "Did God Help Gabrielle Douglas Win?" *Salon*, August 3, 2012, https://www.salon.com/2012/08/03/did_god_help_gabrielle_douglas_win/.

DAY 39 — Ravi Zacharias, Twitter, April 21, 2014, https://twitter.com/ravizacharias/status/458274514926063616?lang=en.

DAY 40 — https://app.first5.org/book/Exodus/ff_exodus_13/.

Sources

DAY 41 — https://www.wow4u.com/anger/.

DAY 42 — Adapted from Stephen Altrogge, *The Greener Grass Conspiracy: Finding Contentment on Your Side of the Fence* (Wheaton, IL: Crossway, 2011).

DAY 43 — https://www.quoteswave.com/picture-quotes/209292.

DAY 44 — https://www.passiton.com/inspirational-quotes/7610-speak-in-such-a-way-that-others-love-to-listen.

DAY 45 — https://www.wiseoldsayings.com/comfort-quotes/.

DAY 46 — https://www.quotes.net/quote/3903.

DAY 47 — https://twitter.com/christinecaine/status/615540233317191680.

DAY 48 — Mark Dever, *Nine Marks of a Healthy Church* (Crossway, 2013), 240.

DAY 49 — http://quotes4sharing.com/2559/.

DAY 50 — Priscilla Shirer, *Awaken: 90 Days With the God Who Speaks* (B&H Books, 2017).

DAY 51 — https://www.scrapbook.com/quotes/doc/14547.html.

DAY 52 — https://www.azquotes.com/quote/680484.

DAY 53 — https://www.brainyquote.com/quotes/camille_pissarro_309695.

DAY 54 — Charles Stanley, *Walking Wisely: Real Life Solutions for Life's Journey* (Nashville: Thomas Nelson, 2002).

DAY 55 — Kay Warren, *Choose Joy: Because Happiness Isn't Enough* (Revell, 2012).

DAY 56 — https://www.azquotes.com/quote/1166244?ref=friendship-with-god.

DAY 57 — John Piper, "How to Preach with Supernatural Power," Bethlehem 2018 Conference for Pastors + Church Leaders, January 17, 2018, https://www.desiringgod.org/messages/how-to-preach-with-supernatural-power.

DAY 58 — https://www.goodreads.com/quotes/858472-what-separates-privilege-from-entitlement-is-gratitude?page=3.

DAY 59 — Author unknown

DAY 60 — Billy Graham, *The Secret of Happiness* (Nashville: Thomas Nelson, 1955, 2002); https://www.ibelieve.com/your-daily-verse/my-home-is-heaven-i-m-just-traveling-through-this-world-billy-graham.html.

FINAL QUOTE: C.S. Lewis, *The Last Battle.* (HarperCollins; Reprint 2002).

Endnotes

[1]Andrew Peterson, "Nothing to Say," ©2001, Provident Label Group, LLC.

[2]Video: https://abcnews.go.com/US/army-dad-surprises-blindfolded-son-martial-arts-class/story?id=61836898.

[3]https://shaunti.com/videos/today-show-shaunti-feldhahn.

[4] Ray Vander Laan, That the World May Know Series with Ray Vander Laan, Volume 12, Walking with God in the Desert—Green Pastures, https://www.youtube.com/watch?v=2x8MwiTs0hM.

[5] JamilynHull.com

[6] "Every life has a story . . . if we only bother to read it," ©2010 Chick-Fil-A, https://vimeo.com/13509635.

[7]James Clear, Atomic Habits: An Easy & Proven Way to Build Good Habits & Break Bad Ones (New York: Avery, 2018), 63.

[8]Henry T. Blackaby and Claude V. King, Experiencing God: Knowing and Doing the Will of God (Lifeway Press, 2007).

[9]Hannah Hurnard, Hinds' Feet on High Places (Carol Stream, IL: Tyndale House, 2017).

[10]Travis Bradberry, Ph.D., "How Complaining Rewires Your Brain for Negativity," https://www.talentsmart.com/articles/How-Complaining-Rewires-Your-Brain-for-Negativity-2147446676-p-1.html.

[11]See Shaunti Feldhahn, The Kindness Challenge (Colorado Springs: Waterbrook, 2016), 63–64.

[12]Harlan Cohen, The Naked Roommate: And 107 Other Issues You Might Run Into in College (Naperville, IL: Sourcebooks, Inc, 2007).

[13]See www.jointhekindnesschallenge.com for a description.

[14]See "Does Venting Anger Feed or Extinguish the Flame?" by Brad Bushman, http://www-personal.umich.edu/~bbushman/PSPB02.pdf, as well as the Psychology Today article about the study: https://www.psychologytoday.com/blog/get-psyched/201309/anger-management-what-works-and-what-doesnt.

[15]See Shaunti Feldhahn, The Surprising Secrets of Highly Happy Marriages (Colorado Springs: Multnomah, 2013), 77–93.

[16]Corrie Ten Boom, Elizabeth Sherrill, John Sherrill, The Hiding Place (Chosen Books, 2006).

[17]C.S. Lewis, The Last Battle (New York: HarperCollins, 2002).